THE BRAND PLAYBOOK

By

Donovan Boyd

The Marketing Coach

Special thanks to Dominique Boyd and Jerome Peterson, Jr.

Ordering & Booking Information:
Special discounts are available on quantity purchases of books by corporations, associations, and others. For ordering details or to book Donovan Boyd for your next speaking engagement, please contact:

booking@marketingismysport.com

1st ed.

ISBN: 978-1-945993-00-8 (print)

Table Of Contents

The Pre-Game

1st Quarter

2nd Quarter

3rd Quarter

4th Quarter

A Message From The Marketing Coach

Are you tired of sitting on the sideline in the game of business and life? It's time to lace up those shoes, put on your uniform, toss those fears aside, and get into the game! The biggest and most intimidating step when getting into business or creating a brand is actually getting started. I believe this is hardest part. You may have a vision, but you don't know where to start. *The Brand Playbook* will walk you through this game, play by play, to help you jumpstart your dream. The simple exercises in this playbook will make you think about your ability as an entrepreneur and give you an idea of how your business will look once you put the wheels in motion. There are a lot of things you may overlook when starting a business and this is why having a playbook is helpful. Even if you have already started a business, you may find that you have skipped some vital steps in the process or need to polish up your practices.

In 2003, I moved from Cleveland, Ohio to New York City to play football for Fordham University. I also was a volunteer coordinator for Russell Simmons and a marketing intern for Atlantic records. Injury ended my marriage with football, and I then fell in love with marketing and entertainment. Being a professional marketer is just like being an athlete; if you want to be the best, you have to train and dedicate your life to your goal. I have always had good jobs working for major corporations, and even though I landed my dream job as head of entertainment for a local casino owned by Caesars Entertainment, it wasn't enough for me because all I was doing was making someone else's dream come true. I could not keep my entrepreneurial spirit from bursting out of me! When I earned my MBA from South University, it showed me that I could accomplish anything that I put my mind to.

It forced me to dig deep inside myself to get to this point and I will continue to push myself towards my dreams. I want to travel the world, share my gift and business knowledge, and help as many brands as possible achieve success. I am blessed due to the amount of people who want to work with me and I am humbled that people trust me with their brands and visions. Marketing is my passion. When I see my ideas come to life, I feel like Kobe hitting a game winner, or A-Rod hitting a 3-run home run to win the game! As a marketing coach, I look at my clients as players, and just like any coach, I want my players to succeed. As a business owner, I want you to understand the importance of developing your brand and how essential it is to execute your game plan.

I know that I have work to do with my brand, and just like any other challenge, it is a constant race, not a sprint. It's a marathon and the one who trains the hardest and puts in those countless hours in the gym will be the one at the finish line. My passion is to help you discover why you're on this journey, what your brand is, why it exists, who will engage in the brand, and how you will touch the world on this journey. The vital goal of this playbook is to get you to understand that you *brand* your business before you *market* your business. We will touch on this more in depth in the playbook, and by the end of the journey you will develop, what I call, a solid brand of value. Many times we see people or companies launch a new product we know nothing about, or an unknown author publish a book, or even come across a new restaurant with no reviews. Too often, people market themselves before they take the time to brand themselves. We think that it's all about marketing and telling everyone that we exist, but before we can get to that point, there are some steps we have to take and work we have to do.

This playbook will teach you the dos and don'ts when it comes to your brand. I want you to put this book down knowing that all aspects of your business have been defined and you have developed a solid and cohesive brand that can be marketed and introduced to the world. I have also included a clipboard for you at the end of each play for you to write down any takeaways that you would like to remember and apply to your business. Take your time with this playbook and really get the most out of these exercises so that you can bring your vision to life and create an engaging brand that individuals will want to be a part of as consumers or as employees. Congratulations on your first step to greatness!

- **Donovan Boyd**

The Marketing Coach

1st Quarter

Play #1

Basic Rules Of The Game

So, what exactly is a brand? Webster defines the word "brand" as a class of goods identified by name as the product of a single firm or manufacturer. Currently when I think of the word "brand" and what it really means, I define it as a complete experience made up of words and visuals. Your brand is your promise to your customers; it lets them know what to expect from what you're offering, whether it's a product or a service. This is what's going to separate you from the competition. Remember that it's who you are and who you are striving to be.

Make sure that your brand message is clear and remember that you cannot be all things to all people. This message has to be clear enough that you can explain it to your employees so that they can duplicate this with your customers. The individuals working for you must be able to turn your brand message into a brand promise so that your customers will continue to frequent your business. Once they do, they will be loyal to your brand via your product or service.

Word & Brand Consistency

The words that you use to identify your brand's unique voice will subsequently define what your brand means to you and your audience. The language you use will also set the tone in which you enter your specific industry. Figuring out your voice is no easy task. When you and your team are working on identifying your voice, you want the message that you're pushing out to be a strong representation of who you are, who your company is, and what your brand is all about. You want to make sure that this is a task that is tackled early on in your process because your voice is going to be a part of what connects you to your consumer. So for example, will your voice be strong, direct, friendly, charming, wise, or witty? Being able to develop content that speaks in this tone to your consumer is ultimately your brand's voice. You start this process by writing out the characteristics of your voice. You do not have to use the same words every time but you want to make sure that the voice is consistently enthused. Also, keep in mind of the industry you're going into. This is a major key because this will be one of the attributes that separates you from other players in your industry. You want your brand's personality to engage or capture the personality of your ideal consumer in your chosen industry.

Once you develop the language of your brand, the culture, and the dynamics of the company, you want to make sure that this language that you're adapting is consistent over the following platforms. This consistency ensures that your brand is creating trust and loyalty with your consumers. Take a look at the platforms below:

→   Webpage Content

→　　Business Card Message

→　　Mission and Vision Statement

→　　Speech/Presentation Language

WORD EXERCISE:

You want to make sure that the consistency of your words spreads across all of your platforms. I let all my clients know that consistency is an important piece of their brand experience; you do not want your customers experiencing something different every time they are patronizing your business. Think of ways you can exercise consistency in the four platforms above. Write an idea for each platform in the space below. Remember, be consistent!

a.　　Webpage Content _____

b.　　Business Card Message _____

c.　　Mission and Vision Statement _____

d.　　Speech/Presentation Language _____

Brand Development

Do not start your business with a name or a logo! First, create a connection with what you're trying to accomplish and the story surrounding your business. Developing your brand's story is important. Remember everyone has a story, whether it's a personal story or a story behind your business. Be sure to include why you got started and why you chose a particular product to sell or service to provide. You want to make a connection with your story and your consumer; you want your consumer to make a connection and relate to your story and in return, buy your product. The product or service is just a bonus to someone buying into and believing in your story. This is how you create brand loyalty. People will be more likely to support your mission if it's something they believe in as much as you do.

BRAND DEVELOPMENT EXERCISE:

In the space provided below, tell your story. Don't be afraid to share your story with others, and remember, people respond to realness and authenticity.

Visuals

A strong brand consists of words and visuals that together equal a guest experience, whether you offer a product or a service. When you think about visuals for your brand, what are some things that bring your vision to life and tell the story of your business to your consumers? For example, colors create a direct connection with your consumers. When you get further along in the stages of growth, even things such as furniture, promo materials, and signage all relay your brand's message visually, which ultimately enhances the customer experience. These are the components that bring your words to life:

→ Artistry - Once you have developed your content, it is time to get creative and develop what this brand will look like and how this brand will stand out from the rest. The more content you have and the clearer your vision of this brand is, the easier it is to develop the artistry. Having a strong graphic designer is key in this process because you want to connect with someone who is a great designer and who you can also communicate well with because this is the person who will bring your brand to life visually.

→ Colors - You want 2-3 colors to represent your brand. Research the meaning of each color and pick a pallet that will accurately represent your brand and that will speak to your target audience. You want these colors to be consistent across all platforms where your brand can be viewed.

→ Materials - These are the things that will bring your vision to three-dimensional life. Thinking about these things will enhance the experience of your clients when they frequent your establishment. Promotional material is another way to make a connection between your client and your brand. Materials can include pens, pop-up banners, flyers, even down to the furniture that you have in your establishment. For example, if the color of your logo is red, your materials could be red couches, signage, fixtures or any other items that can burn the image of your brand in your client's mind. The goal is Brand, Brand, and Brand some more.

When you think about the word "brand", I want you to think about what your business stands for, its beliefs, and its core values. I want you to take pride in your brand because it will be how people relate to you when you're not in the room. Why did you start on this journey? Why does this product or service exist? When I think about my journey and how I fell in love with marketing 10 years ago, and seeing how the industry has changed, it fascinates me. When I got injured in college and my NFL dreams ended, it was marketing that allowed me to still be creative and train to be the best at something. I did not know where this journey would lead me, but I wanted to help as many brands as possible from major corporations, to start-ups and entrepreneurs. I believed that I could unlock brand potential and assist brands in reaching the audiences they sought.

Business Logo

A logo is a recognizable and distinctive graphic design, stylized name, or unique symbol that identifies your business. If you are not a graphic designer, then I highly recommend finding one in your local area who can bring your brand vision to life. There are many ways to find a designer. Start the research process on social media or ask someone in your network to recommend someone they know or have worked with in the past. Make sure that you see their work beforehand. You need someone who has the style you are going for and is easy to work with because you will use this designer for the majority of your company content and collateral.

In most cases, your potential clients will come across your logo first before they ever see your product or learn anything about your services. Your first impression is a lasting impression, so you want to make sure that your potential consumer falls totally in love with your brand just by looking at your logo.

Even though this is the first representation of your company to the world, this is not the first thing you want to come up with when starting on this journey. I encourage you to discover your brand story first, as well as everything we discussed that goes along with that. Developing your brand first will make it so much easier to come up with a logo because you will already have the foundation laid. Coming up with a logo is not a step that you want to skip because it is very important when you think about brand recognition. The consumer will come across your logo more than they come across your products or services, so make sure that your foundation backs up the great logo. Once you have that great logo, you want to make sure that it is present on all your content, as well as any other thing surrounding your brand such as sponsorship opportunities, advertisement, promo material, and more.

LOGO QUESTIONNAIRE EXERCISE:

Coming up with a logo and deciding how it will represent the brand is a very important step in the entire branding process. Below are some questions to get your thought process going:

1. What is the name that you will be using on your logo?

2. Who is your target audience?

3. Describe your selected industry.

4.   What would you say is the style of your brand?

_____

_____

_____

_____

5.   What are some examples of logos that you like? (send these to your designer)

_____

_____

_____

_____

6.   Where will your logo be mostly displayed? (business cards, website, signage, t-shirt, etc.)

_____

_____

_____

_____

7.   What colors would you like to see on your logo?

_____

_____

_____

_____

8.   List characteristics that describe the look and feel of your desired logo (simple, modern, luxurious, feminine, complex).

_____

_____

_____

_____

In order to ensure that you have the best representation of your brand, I want you to assess the design of your logo and ask yourself the following questions:

1.   *Do I feel that my logo design accurately reflects the personality of my organization?*

2.   *Is the logo easily readable from far away?*

3.   *How timeless is my logo design?*

4.   *What is the overall feeling I get when I look at my new logo design?*

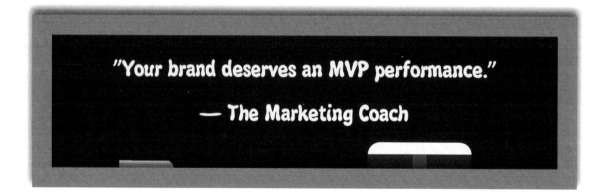

Mission Statement

The next thing to do is formulate a mission statement. Your mission Statement is an operative description of what your company or organization does. Your team should have clear direction of what the focus of the company is after reading the mission statement. If you think about any professional sports team, the mission or goal is clear: to compete for and win a championship! Below are examples of mission statements from major global companies:

Nike Mission Statement:
"Bring Inspiration And Innovation To Every Athlete In The World. If You Have A Body, You Are An Athlete."

The Marketing Coach Mission Statement:
"My mission is to help businesses & individuals unlock their brand potential through innovative strategies that create brand value & aid customer loyalty."

Google's Mission Statement:
"...to organize the world's information and make it universally accessible and useful."

NFL Mission Statement:
"To provide our fans, communities, and partners the highest quality sports and entertainment in the world, and to do so in a way that is consistent with our values."

MISSION STATEMENT EXERCISE:

Create your mission statement below.

_____

_____

_____

_____

Vision Statement

When it comes to the vision for the team and the organization, I want you to create BIGGER GOALS that you can think of for your company! The vision allows people to understand the direction in which the company is headed and to make sure that the vision is clear and concise. See below examples of vision statements from other companies:

Special Olympics Vision Statement:
"To transform communities by inspiring people throughout the world to open their minds, accept and include people with intellectual disabilities, and thereby anyone who is perceived as different."

Cleveland Clinic Vision Statement:
"Striving to be the world's leader in patient experience, clinical outcomes, research, and education."

Nike Vision Statement:
"To be the number one athletic company in the world."

VISION STATEMENT EXERCISE:

Create your vision statement below.

_____

_____

_____

_____

_____

Company Tagline

Your company tagline is a catchy phrase that is used to make your brand stand out in the minds of the people. Your tagline, sometimes referred to as a slogan, is sometimes attached to a logo, the bottom of your business card or website, or often used at the end of a TV or radio commercial. For example, at the end of every Motel 6 commercial, you hear their tag line: "We'll leave the light on for you." For The Marketing Coach brand, my tagline is "Marketing is My Sport." You must keep your tagline consistent with your brand if you decide to use one. Taglines are very helpful in terms of brand awareness.

TAGLINE EXERCISE:

Create your tagline below.

_____

_____

_____

_____

_____

_____

Core Values

Core values are the philosophies in which your organization does business internally and externally (i.e. respect, responsibility, etc.). Your core values should represent your culture and who you are as an organization. They are the values your company is built upon.

CORE VALUES EXERCISE:

What would you say are your core values? List 5 below.

1. _____

2. _____

3. _____

4. _____

5. _____

Standard Operating Procedures

In this day and age, customer experiences are the driving force in brand loyalty. You have to develop Standard Operating Procedures (SOPs) so that this experience is the best and remains consistent at all times, no matter who is dealing with your customers. The SOPs will outline everything, step by step, so that there is no discrepancy on how to do anything within your business. This is a good tool to use because it allows you, as a business owner, to hold people accountable. There should be no reason why an employee says that they do not know how to do something if you sit down with your team and develop these procedures.

The first business I started was an artist management and marketing company in 2010. I skipped a lot of these steps because I was eager to get my business off of the ground. I connected with a graphic designer and created a logo, a website, and got to work. However, my brand was not consistent across the board because I didn't take the time to address and develop these areas of my business. We were making music and putting out decent visuals and content, but it was not enough to establish a brand. It was not until I started researching my industry and educating myself on what I needed for my business that I realized what I should have been doing all along. I thought we were making moves because we had logos, business cards, and a website, but the colors were not the same and the logos were different because I had multiple people working on this for me, which did not allow for us to put out consistent content. I learned a lot from the experience, and this is now a part of my foundation of coaching my clients because I have bumped my head a few times and have been in their shoes. If there were SOPs in place, a lot of these headaches could have been avoided.

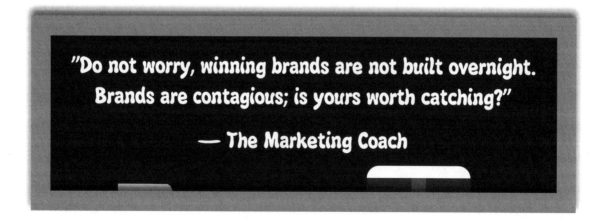

"Do not worry, winning brands are not built overnight. Brands are contagious; is yours worth catching?"

— The Marketing Coach

Brand Personality

Webster defines "personality" as the complex of characteristics that distinguishes an individual, nation, or group; especially the totality of an individual's behavioral and emotional characteristics. As you are developing your brand, I want you to always stay aware of your brand personality. Just like you have a personality, your brand does too, and it is important that this personality is one that customers are going to want to be around. You have to always be mindful of the impression your brand is leaving on your audience. Your brand's personality is a determining factor in your brand and customer loyalty.

BRAND PERSONALITY EXERCISE:

This exercise will expand on how you want your brand to interact with your customer.

1.   How does your brand behave?

   _____

   _____

   _____

   _____

   _____

   _____

2.   How are you a representation of your brand?

   _____

   _____

   _____

   _____

   _____

   _____

3. How do you live the life your brand represents?

_____

_____

_____

_____

_____

_____

4. How does your brand stay connected with your consumers?

_____

_____

_____

_____

_____

_____

5. What experience does your brand create?

_____

_____

_____

_____

_____

_____

6.   How does your brand make people feel?

_____

_____

_____

_____

_____

7.   How does your brand look to the public?

_____

_____

_____

_____

_____

Brand Culture

A brand culture is who you are as a company and what you believe in as a company. Your culture should be contagious so that everyone catches it. But remember, you cannot deter from it because that will show inconsistency. Your culture will be the ideals on which you firmly stand on and by which you live as an entire organization.

You want your culture to be authentic and organic, but the following exercise will help spark ideas to start you on a path of developing a culture for your brand or company.

BRAND CULTURE EXERCISE:

1. Who are you as a company?

_____

_____

_____

_____

_____

_____

2. What is your business philosophy?

_____

_____

_____

_____

_____

_____

3. What principles will you stand on as a company?

_____

_____

_____

_____

_____

_____

_____

4.   What is your company's way of life?

_____

_____

_____

_____

_____

5.   How do your employees or team fit into your culture?

_____

_____

_____

_____

_____

6.   What is the plan to implement the culture?

_____

_____

_____

_____

_____

7. Once you have a culture implemented, how do you maintain and enforce this way of life?

_____

_____

_____

_____

_____

8. What is your plan for communicating this to the entire organization?

_____

_____

_____

_____

_____

9. What does your culture say about the environment?

_____

_____

_____

_____

_____

_____

Brand Pillars

When you think the of the word "pillar", you think about a statue or a strong piece of material that is holding a building in place. That pillar is a part of the foundation of that building; without it, the building could not stand. So when thinking about your brand, you need to establish pillars that your company is built upon. These pillars are non-negotiable; they will always be a part of the interior and exterior of your business. With most buildings, the pillars stand out and are used as a talking piece or focal point of the building. When answering these questions below, keep in mind that this will be the reason why people choose your brand and why it will stand out against your competitors in the market. Below are questions that will help you determine what those pillars are.

BRAND PILLARS EXERCISE:

1.   Why did you create your company or brand?

_____

_____

_____

_____

_____

_____

2.   When it comes to business, what is important to you?

_____

_____

_____

_____

_____

_____

3. How do you want your brand to be identified? What is your brand identity?

_____

_____

_____

_____

_____

_____

4. What is the location of your business? How much research have your done on this location? How important is location in the success of your business?

_____

_____

_____

_____

_____

_____

5. What kind of work environment would you like your employees to be a part of?

_____

_____

_____

_____

_____

_____

Social Media & Hashtags

When it comes to social media, the biggest question that people have is, "Should I have a business page versus a personal page, or should I have both?" The answer to this question depends upon the nature of your brand or business. If you are selling a product or service, it is very important that you have a business page. Since it's a free platform, you want to make sure you are utilizing these services to push your brand and business because you want it to be clear who your audience is and who is interested in your product or service. When you have a business page, social media allows you to target those who are following you or show interest in your business with ads.

I do not encourage you to turn your personal page into a business page or constantly advertise your business on your personal page. You can encourage them to head over to your business page and follow that page for the latest updates on your company. That way, there is a distinct difference between the two pages. It gets tricky if you embody the business or the brand. I would advise you to do a social media audit to get rid of things that do not fall in line with your brand on your personal page. If you're using social media to push your personal brand, then this is a step that you need to do. For example, if you are a speaker, life coach, or author, and you want to use this platform, then you want to leave the personal things off of your social media because those posts can come back to haunt you. I advise my clients to always be conscious of what they do on social media as it pertains to their business and personal lives. I know this is not easy, but you have to make it clear which avenues you are going to use because what you do on your personal pages can affect your brand or business.

Another important thing to think about on social media are hashtags. Hashtags are key because they allow for your message to live on after your original post. Hashtags are one of the best ways to gain exposure on social media. I look at it as free advertising when used on a consistent basis. Hashtags are a great way to get your content in front of other like-minded individuals and draw attention to your page. Simple tags can lend credibility to your brand based on what surrounds it. The tags that you use should be based on what your ideal client is seeking. You can even take it a step further and ask yourself what would someone Google search to find a business similar to yours. Those are the tags you want to start with first. When you have these down, come up with your own hashtags that are branded specifically for your business. These can be consistent with your tagline, company name, campaign, or website name. There is nothing wrong with having several that you can call your own.

You can use up to 30 hashtags per Instagram post, but when building your following, you want to make sure that you are always using 5-15 tags per post once you have determined which ones are going to work best for you. It takes time to understand which ones will work best for your page, so keep in mind that you need to monitor the engagement and responses that you get on your posts to determine if you are using the appropriate hashtags. When conducting online research on hashtags in your industry or what your customer is searching, stick to hashtags that have between 5,000 to 500,000 posts. You want to avoid the tags that have over 1 million posts (unless the engagement for your page is through the roof), otherwise your page will get lost in the masses.

SOCIAL MEDIA EXERCISE:

For branding purposes, choosing a company name on social media is key because you want to make sure that you can have consistent social media handles across all these platforms below. List the business name you plan to use for each outlet.

1.   Instagram: _____

2.   Facebook: _____

3.   Twitter: _____

4.   Snapchat: _____

5.   YouTube: _____

6.   Periscope: _____

7.   LinkedIn: _____

HASHTAG EXERCISE: Below, create your unique custom hashtags.

Researched Hashtags (Relevant Trending Tags):

1. #_____
2. #_____
3. #_____
4. #_____
5. #_____
6. #_____
7. #_____
8. #_____

Branded Hashtags (Custom Tag):

1. #_____
2. #_____
3. #_____
4. #_____
5. #_____
6. #_____
7. #_____
8. #_____

Industry Hashtags:

1. #_____
2. #_____
3. #_____

HASHTAG AUDIT EXERCISE: Hashtag Audit

1. If you're currently already using Instagram or outlets that utilize tags, what are the top 5 hashtags that you are currently using? Write the hashtags below, search them on your social media platform, and write down the number of posts for each hashtag.

#_____ Number of Posts_____

#_____ Number of Posts_____

#_____ Number of Posts_____

#_____ Number of Posts_____

#_____ Number of Posts_____

2.   Based off of the data above, are any of your posts standing out on these pages?

_____

_____

_____

_____

_____

_____

3.   How can you better define your hashtags so that they stand out on your desired pages?

_____

_____

_____

_____

_____

_____

Let's Recap!

This play is intended to help you develop a brand standard for your organization. Once you have established the foundational guidelines, these standards can be packaged and rolled out through the entire company, no matter how large or small.

Make sure that you are not developing everything yourself. It is valuable to get a second opinion or have a team of people that can come up with the answers to all of these questions. External input ensures that the branding is perceived the same way across a diverse group and has the consumer in mind!

TAKEAWAYS:

Play #2

If You Don't Play To Succeed, You Play To Fail!

Disclaimer: The information contained after the first paragraph in this section is directly from www.sba.gov. Information provided from a government site is considered public domain and not subject to copyright laws. This information is being provided as a resource and is not intended to depict the original writing of the author. For detailed information about business plans and the services the Small Business Administration offers, please visit their website.

Unless you have an amazing gift of entrepreneurship and can create and run a successful business on a whim, you will need a business plan. A business plan is crucial for starting and running your business successfully. Sound business plans can help you get a loan, keep you on track toward your goals, and provide a reference for benchmarking, reviewing results, and making adjustments in your business. The United States Small Business Association provides a great template for how to write a business plan by section. Every business plan should include, at minimum, the following sections: Executive Summary, Company Description, Market Analysis, Organization & Management, Service or Product Line (description), Marketing & Sales (strategy), Funding Requirements (requests), Financial Projections, and Appendices.

The following area only goes over the basic descriptions of the sections within a business plan provided on their website. It is best to go on www.sba.gov for more information.

Executive Summary. The executive summary is often considered the most important section of a business plan. This section briefly tells your reader where your company is, where you want to take it, and why your business idea will be successful. If you are seeking financing, the executive summary is also your first opportunity to grab a potential investor's interest. The executive summary should highlight the strengths of your overall plan and therefore be the last section you write. However, it usually appears first in your business plan document.

Company Description. This section of your business plan provides a high-level review of the different elements of your business. This is similar to an extended elevator pitch and can help readers and potential investors quickly understand the goal of your business and its unique proposition. It includes the nature of your business, your marketplace, the products and services, etc.

Market Analysis. The market analysis section of your business plan should illustrate your industry and market knowledge as well as any of your research findings and conclusions. This section is usually presented after the company description. It includes a description of your industry and the outlook in terms of supply and demand.

Organization & Management. This section should include your company's organizational structure, details about the ownership of your company, profiles of your management team, and the qualifications of your board of directors. Who does what in your business? What is their background and why are you bringing them into the business as board members or employees?

Service or Product Line. This is where you describe your service or product, emphasizing the benefits to potential and current customers. Focus on why your particular product will fulfill a need for your target customers.

Marketing & Sales Management. The first thing you want to do in this section is define your marketing strategy. There is no single way to approach a marketing strategy; your strategy should be part of an ongoing business-evaluation process and unique to your company.

Funding Request. If you are seeking funding for your business venture, use this section to outline your requirements. Your funding request should include the following information:

➜ Your current funding requirement.

➜ Any future funding requirements over the next five years.

➜ How do you intend to use the funds you receive: Is the funding request for capital expenditures?

➜ Working capital? Debt retirement? Acquisitions? Whatever it is, be sure to list it in this section.

➜ Any strategic financial situational plans for the future (i.e. a buyout, being acquired, debt repayment plan, or selling your business)? These areas are extremely important to a future creditor, since they will directly impact your ability to repay your loan(s).

Financial Prospectus. This section should include historical financial data about your company if applicable. If the company is a start-up, this section should include what you expect your company to be able to do within the next year, two years, and five years. Make sure your projections match your funding requests.

Appendix. The appendix should be provided to readers on an as-needed basis. It will include necessary information like your credit history, product pictures, letters of reference, legal documents, etc. In other words, it should not be included with the main body of your business plan. Your plan is your communication tool and will be seen by a lot of people. Some of the information in the business section you will not want everyone to see, but specific individuals (such as creditors) may want access to this information to make lending decisions.

Any copies of your business plan should be controlled, so keep a distribution record to keep track of who you have sent it to. This will allow you to update and maintain your business plan on an as-needed basis. Also remember that you should include a private placement disclaimer with your business plan if you plan to use it to raise capital.

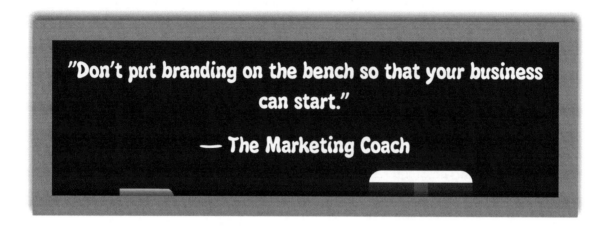

BUSINESS PLAN EXERCISE:

1. Develop the outline for your business plan including the first eight (8) sections. Provide two or three paragraphs summarizing each section of the business plan using your personal planning for your business. For Business Plan templates go to: http://www.sbdcnet.org/small-business-information-center/business-plans

    a. Executive Summary

    _____

    _____

    _____

    _____

    _____

    _____

b.   Company Description

_____

_____

_____

_____

_____

_____

c.   Market Analysis

_____

_____

_____

_____

_____

_____

d.   Organization & Management

_____

_____

_____

_____

_____

_____

e.   Service or Product Line

_____

_____

_____

_____

f.   Marketing & Sales Management

_____

_____

_____

_____

g.   Funding Request

_____

_____

_____

_____

h.   Financial Plan (Prospectus)

_____

_____

_____

_____

_____

_____

_____

2.   Forecast and list five (5) goals for your business at the five-year mark. At this point, an organization should show strong growth and maturity.

➜   _____

➜   _____

➜   _____

➜   _____

➜   _____

3.   What cost savings can you utilize to reduce your marketing cost? Think of ten (10) ways to use your networks and partnerships?

➜   _____

➜   _____

➜   _____

➜   _____

➜   _____

→ _____

→ _____

→ _____

→ _____

→ _____

4. If you've completed your business plan, create a PowerPoint presentation that will summarize the key points of your plan to potential investors and lenders. What key points will you include?

_____

_____

_____

_____

_____

_____

Let's Recap!

Great teams play hard, not just to participate, but to succeed! However, that success is driven by a detailed plan of attack. A business owner must create an executable plan or they risk losing when it counts the most!

TAKEAWAYS:

Play #3

Team Firsts

It is such a great feeling to be in a position to start your own business! However, some decide to execute before they plan and prepare. But preparing is not just developing a business plan, it's actually assessing if you have the correct mindset to start your business by understanding your business structure and setting up the appropriate business related accounts. A potential business owner must also assess or employ someone that understands the laws and regulations related to your business, as well as the possible tax implications of starting the business.

This reminds me of one of my first potential clients. He had an amazing "life hack" that consisted of repurposing old ties. While I won't get into the specifics of his trade, I felt it was a great idea and I had him meet me at a local coffee shop to discuss how he could best utilize my services. The conversation was going well until we got into a discussion to determine what foundational operational activities he'd already completed. The checklist went something like this:

Business Name?
"No"

Business Structure?
"What is that?"

Tax ID?
"No"

Business Account?
"No"

Vendor's License?
"Do I need a license?"

Are there any laws that govern selling repurposed products?
"No…well, I don't know."

The gentleman wrapped up the meeting by handing me a business card he wrote out on a torn piece of a paper bag! At this point, I knew I needed to intervene as soon as possible. He was already selling these repurposed ties and ruining his product and brand reputation; it was totally unprofessional. I ended the meeting with the assignment to perform a self-assessment of his personal abilities to run a successful business as well as help him build the necessary foundation to run his business. If you are already in the execution phase and haven't adequately developed your foundation, consider the following steps:

#1: Self-Assessment

One of the first things you should do before you start your own company is to assess the reason why you want to be in business for yourself in the first place. Starting your own business is a daunting task, but it is an exciting and rewarding experience. There are many benefits to entrepreneurship, such as being your own boss, developing your own schedule, and earning a living doing something you love and enjoy. However, being successful at any venture requires thorough planning, creativity, and hard work. Many people want to start their own businesses, but most are simply not equipped to do so. There are some characteristics and skill sets that most successful entrepreneurs share. If you fall in line with any of the following, it could lead to success:

→ *Be comfortable taking risks.* One drawback (if you want to call it that) to being your own boss is that you're the lone person responsible for making crucial, tough decisions. Entrepreneurship involves uncertainty. Are you completely risk adverse? If yes, then entrepreneurship probably isn't a good fit for you. Do you feel comfortable taking calculated risks?

→ *Independent.* You are the primary decision maker, so you will need to trust your instincts. Additionally, you have to be willing to accept an occasional "no" (well actually, quite a few of them). You have to be confident in knowing that behind every "no", there's a lesson that leads to a "yes".

→ *Persuasive.* You may have the greatest product or service in the world, but if you cannot persuade customers, employees, and potential lenders or partners to believe in your product or service, you may find entrepreneurship to be challenging. Some of the best entrepreneurs are the greatest persuaders. You need to be able to lead and convince others that you have a great product or service and that it's worth buying, developing, or selling.

→ *Master negotiator.* As a small business owner, everything is up for negotiation! The terms of the lease for your building space, the cost of contracted product development, the cost of materials—everything will need to be negotiated for the sake of your business. Great negotiation skills will help you save money and keep your business running smoothly.

→ *Creativity.* Every business owner needs to be creative. Doing something different and innovative is one of the primary reasons most individuals decide to start businesses. Can you imagine new ways to solve problems? Entrepreneurs must be able to think creatively.

→ *Have the support of others.* Before you start a business, it's important to have a strong support system in place. You'll be forced to make many important decisions, especially in the first months of opening your business. It's important to have a business mentor or someone to hold you accountable and someone you can bounce ideas off of that will give you constructive feedback.

#2: Opening Up a Business Account

Every business should have a business account — separate from the owner's personal account. Opening a business bank account is simple now that most banks allow you to set up an account online. Most often, the process is simple but requires certain documentation based on the type of business you are opening. So, what type of documentation is required to open a business bank account online? Marco Carbajo, owner of the blog website www.businesscreditblogger.com, wrote a great article that provided a list of all the documents needed to opening a business account based on the legal business structure. Additionally, definitions were provided so you can understand, at minimum, each business structure.

Sole Proprietorship - A Sole Proprietor is someone who owns an unincorporated business by himself or herself. If you are the sole owner of a limited liability company, you are also considered a sole proprietorship or disregarded entity, unless you choose to treat your LLC as a corporation.

You will need:

→ Social Security Number or Business Tax Identification Number

→ Business License showing both business and owner's name, or

→ Business name filing document, such as a Fictitious Name Certificate or Certificate of Trade Name, showing both business and owner's name

General Partnership - A General Partnership is an arrangement in which partners conducting a business cooperatively have unlimited liability, which means their personal assets are liable to the partnership's obligations.

You will need:

→ Business Tax Identification Number

→ Partnership Agreement showing business name and name of partners, and

➜ Business name filing document, such as Fictitious Name Certificate or Certificate of Trade Name, showing business name and name of partners

Limited Partnership - A Limited Partnership (LP) is a form of partnership similar to a general partnership, except that a general partnership must have at least two General Partners (GPs), whereas a limited partnership must have at least one GP and at least one limited partner.

You will need:

➜ Business Tax Identification Number

➜ Limited Partnership Agreement showing business name and name of partners, and

➜ Business organizing document filed with and certified by state official, such as Certificate of Limited Partnership, showing business name and name of partners

Limited Liability Company - A Limited Liability Company (LLC) is the United States-specific form of a private limited company. It is a business structure that combines the pass-through taxation of a partnership or sole proprietorship with the limited liability of a corporation.

You will need:

➜ Business Tax Identification Number

➜ Articles of Organization or Certificate of Formation

➜ Corporate Resolution identifying authorized signers if the officer names are not listed on Articles of Organization or Certificate of Formation

Limited Liability Partnership - A Limited Liability Partnership (LLP) is a partnership in which some or all partners (depending on the jurisdiction) have limited liabilities. It therefore exhibits elements of partnerships and corporations. In an LLP, one partner is not responsible or liable for another partner's misconduct or negligence.

You will need:

➜ Business Tax Identification Number

➔ Limited Liability Partnership Agreement showing business name and name of partners, and

➔ Business organizing document filed and certified by a state official, such as Certificate of Limited Liability Partnership, showing the business name and name of partners

Corporation - A Corporation is a legal entity that is separate and distinct from its owners. Corporations enjoy most of the rights and responsibilities that an individual possesses; that is, a corporation has the right to enter into contracts, loan and borrow money, sue and be sued, hire employees, own assets, and pay taxes.

You will need:[1]

➔ Business Tax Identification Number

➔ Articles of Incorporation or Certificate of Incorporation

➔ Corporate Resolution identifying authorized signers if the officer names are not listed on Articles of Incorporation or Certificate of Incorporation

#3 Choose a Name and Register Your Business

The name of my company is The Boyd Group, LLC and my website is www.theboydgroupllc.com. When I was coming up with the name of my company, which specializes in marketing, branding, and management services, I wanted a name that was tied into my personal name but wouldn't make potential clients think that I was only a marketing company. I sought advice from mentors and other professionals because feedback is key, and I learned that I needed a name that would allow me to expand in other industries if I wanted to. I wanted my name to be distinguished and synonymous with excellence. I ended up going with the word "group" because that word always reminded me of law firms or insurance companies, but when I saw the word in a company name, it gave me the feeling that they mean business.

I encourage you to not rush this process, take your time and come up with a name that you truly feel represents your brand. Make sure that this is something you attack early on because this is the starting point of your journey. This name will need to connect with the audience you are trying to speak to in

---

[1] *For more information, go to https:www.sba.gov/blogs/how-to-open-small-business-bank-account-online*

the short term and in the long term. Some people may push you towards a trendy name or a fancy name, but think about a name that is unique and timeless. Lastly, make sure that there is a meaning behind the name, then marketing can showcase this meaning in order to connect with your audience.

The selection of a business name is one of the most important things you're going to do for your business. It should align with your brand identity, and you should make sure that you have properly registered and protected your business name.

Choosing a name also means ensuring you haven't chosen a name that someone is already using. It is imperative to check with the US Patent and Trademark Office to search for similar name variations so that you can be sure that no one has your business name and can protect it accordingly. Registering your business name means that you're setting up a "doing business as" (DBA) name. This is the name that you will get protected.

The internet dominates our world, so it's important to choose a name that can easily be used on the web. You want to claim your domain name so your business name will have to be unique or you will have to attach a prefix or suffix so that it can be used. You can simply search for your business name on the internet to see if a webpage pops up.

#4 Research Business Laws

As a small business owner, you are subject to some of the laws and regulations that apply to large corporations. You are an entrepreneur, not a lawyer! What is even more complicated is the amount of laws and regulations that exists for businesses. Some laws and regulations only apply to large corporations and not small businesses and vice versa. There are many laws that relate to businesses. Below are some of the laws you may want to research for your particular industry to see which ones may be important for your business:

→ Advertising and Marketing Law – The Federal Trade Commission (FTC) provides oversight and regulates the advertising and marketing law in the United States. These laws will affect how you "cold-call" people, label products, and governs how you list ingredients if you have a product that you're selling.

→ Employment and Labor Law – Unless you plan on operating your business with only contractors, labor laws will always affect a company. Meeting minimum wage requirements and abiding by anti-discrimination and anti-harassment laws are important to keep any company out of the courthouse.

→ <u>Finance Law</u> - Antitrust, bankruptcy, and securities laws protect the financial interests of small businesses and individual investors.

→ <u>Intellectual Property Law</u> – These laws protect your innovations, logos, ideas, business names, and inventions. The US Patent and Trademark office provides information on how to protect your intellectual property, but I would advise you seek out legal counsel to ensure you properly protect one of your most important assets.

→ <u>Online Business Law</u> – If you've started an online business, these laws will govern how you sell products online as well as when you collect sales tax.

→ <u>Privacy Law</u> – When you're dealing with customers, you're most likely keeping a database of your consumer base. It is important to protect their information by properly securing it or disposing of it when necessary.

→ <u>Workplace Safety and Health Law</u> – It is important to focus on the well-being of your employees. All companies are governed by Occupational Safety and Health Act (OSHA) regulations in that they must create a workplace that is free from hazards that can cause physical danger or death.

#5 Explore State Business Licenses and Regulations

Depending on the type of business you decide to run, you will need certain federal and state licenses and abide by the regulations that govern those licenses. For example, a truck driver needs certain endorsements added to their driver's licenses that enable them to transport people, hazardous materials, and other things. A beautician/barber needs to have their skills certified by a state board to receive a license in cosmetology or a barber's license to legally run their business.

#6 Identify Federal Licenses & Permits

If your business is involved in activities supervised and regulated by a federal agency – such as selling alcohol, firearms, commercial fishing, etc. – you may need to obtain a federal license or permit. Below is a brief list of business activities that require these forms and information on how to apply. In addition, you can also discover which general business permits, licenses, and registrations are required by your state, county or city. If your industry is not listed below, Google it to see what licenses and permits govern your field!

Agriculture: www.aphis.usda.gov/permits

Commercial Fisheries : www.nmfs.noaa.gov/sfa

Alcoholic Beverages: www.ttb.gov

Maritime Transportation: www.fmc.gov/resources

Aviation: www.faa.gov

Radio and Television Broadcasting: www.fcc.gov/encyclopedia

Firearms, Ammunition and Explosives: www.atf.gov

Transportation and Logistics: http://www.ops.fhwa.dot.gov/freight/sw/permit_reportw

Fish and Wildlife: www.fws.gov/permits

7 Determine Tax Implications

One of the first things a company should do is get an Employer Identification Number (EIN) or a Federal Tax Identification Number. This is how the IRS identifies you as a business entity.

Tax implications are unique to each business based on the legal structure (sole proprietor, LLC, LLP, etc.). What is important for most businesses is determining what constitutes an accounting event (or business activity) and that determination will govern the tax.

In general, business owners can deduct what is considered ordinary and necessary expenses needed to conduct business. An ordinary expense is an expense that is common for the nature of business in the industry of the business owner. A necessary expense is appropriate for the business. An example of a necessary expense would be operating expenses for a company. Generally, an accounting event or business activity exists when you enter into that activity with the idea of making a profit. There are some factors that should be considered when attempting to make that determination, they are as follows:

➔ Does the time and effort put into the activity show intent to make or maximize profit?

➔ Does the business depend on revenue from the activity?

➔ If losses exist, are they the result of circumstances beyond the business' control or did they occur during the start-up phase of the business?

➔ Has the business altered operation methods to improve profitability?

→ Does the business or its advisors have the knowledge needed to address the going concern of the business or make the activity sustainable?

→ Does the activity make a profit in some years?

→ Can the business expect to make a profit in the future from the appreciation of assets used in the activity?

The IRS presumes that an activity is performed for profit if it makes a profit during at least three of the last five tax years, including the current year. A business' activities are equal to its product or service. When you understand what your business offers, you may find that you offer more or less products or services than you originally planned for and your taxes should take that into consideration.

Nearly every state imposes a business or corporate income tax. Like federal taxes, your state tax requirement depends on the legal structure of your business. For example, if your business is an LLC, the LLC is taxed separately from the owners of the business, while sole proprietors report their personal and business income taxes using the same form used to report their business taxes.

"Branding beats talent when talent doesn't brand."

— The Marketing Coach

KEY FUNDAMENTALS EXERCISE:

1. Perform your own self-assessment. Write down your strengths and weaknesses in each of the seven areas we previously discussed.

    _____

    _____

    _____

    _____

    _____

    _____

2. Determine what your business' legal structure will be from the list provided (e.g. sole proprietorship, LLC, LLP, etc.). Create a checklist to ensure you have all of the documents necessary to open your business account.

    _____

    _____

    _____

    _____

    _____

    _____

3. Research the various business laws we listed. Write down which ones apply to your business. If these laws create some roadblocks for starting, describe what those roadblocks are and describe how you will overcome them.

    _____

    _____

_____

_____

_____

_____

4.   Research the various licenses we listed or search to see if your business has specific ones not listed. Write down which ones apply to your business. If these licenses create some roadblocks for starting, describe what those roadblocks are and describe how you will overcome them.

_____

_____

_____

_____

_____

Let's Recap!

Is there a difference between planning and preparing? Yes! Teams draft executable game plans and strategies, then they go out on the field to practice and prepare for game time. With an executable business plan, now it's time to prepare your business by attaining the basic and necessary infrastructure to prepare the company for game time!

TAKEAWAYS:

2nd Quarter

Play #4

Are You Worth The Price?

Pricing your business' products represents one of the biggest challenges most start-ups face. Most businesses fail at this point because they don't realize the science of effective pricing. Yes, there's a science to it, and it's not just based on having the largest profit margin. This is especially true when your product is innovative and can't be benchmarked against similar products.

Getting this crucial business element right from the beginning should be one of your top priorities as a start-up owner. There's always a temptation to set prices high to gain the most profit share, but doing that doesn't consider demand. Then there's a known strategy of setting prices low to enter the market, but that's not always effective and can be a hindrance. Pricing low makes future growth less sustainable. It also devalues your product. Consumers are willing to pay a premium for quality products or services. Low-balling yourself doesn't speak to the quality of your product, and low pricing can be hard to recover from as you will eventually have to raise your prices and your customers may not consider the move justifiable.

Back to the science! Well, maybe not a science, but definitely a calculation based on adequate research and looking at three main tangible variables that affect the setting of your prices: Materials Costs, Labor Costs, and Overhead Costs.

→ Materials Costs - The amount of money you spend on the raw materials needed to create your products. If you make/manufacture products, these costs will be fairly straightforward.

→ Labor Costs - The number of hours required to make your product and the hourly rate associated with those hours. It is important to know how much time should go into making your product or providing your service without overtime. Contracted services should also be included in this cost for anything that has been outsourced.

→ Overhead Costs - The administrative expenses not directly related to the manufacturing of your product or service but necessary for the operation of your business. Those expenses would be utilities, administrative expenses for secretaries, and other general office expenses.

Once you've determined a number for these expenses, or at least an appropriate estimate, the following formulas can be used to estimate your prices:

Base Costs = Materials Costs + Labor Costs

Wholesale Costs = (Materials Costs + Labor Costs) x Wholesale Markup

$$\text{Retail Costs} = \text{Wholesale Costs} \ \times \ \text{Retail Markup}$$

$$\text{Profit} = (\text{Retail Markup} \ \times \ \text{Items Sold}) - \text{Overhead Costs}$$

We went over the calculations, but this is where the science comes in. While the math has been determined, there are also a few additional things to consider when coming up with a consumer price:

→ **Research your potential markups.** There are markups that you will be able to charge based on the industry you operate in, so it's worth doing some research into what your niche's standards are.

→ **Respect industry ranges.** If your calculations put your estimated prices significantly above or below your competitors, you need to either adjust your profit margin expectations or find a way to make your products more efficiently. Alternatively, you may be able to add some innovation to your product or find a way to market your product differently in order to command higher prices.

→ **Use these calculations to work backwards to your desired profit.** Try establishing a benchmark for your profit margin in advance before developing costs and prices. This will allow you to obtain a quick preview into the sustainability of your company's product or service.

By using these calculations to develop your costs along with the science of developing your price within your industry, it is possible to set your prices in a way that both attracts potential customers and ensures your start-up's financial stability from the start.

"Your brand needs you to take game-winning shots."

— The Marketing Coach

PRICING EXERCISE:

1. Why should people buy your product or service?

    _____

    _____

    _____

    _____

    _____

    _____

2. Is your product or service considered a niche? Niche products or services normally aim to satisfy a specific area of interest, demographic, price, and quality. Be sure to give this consideration throughout the remainder of the questions.

    _____

    _____

    _____

    _____

    _____

    _____

3. Determine what your materials cost will be for your product or service. You may have materials cost whether or not you develop a product or a service. For example, barbers' materials cost would include alcohol, towels, powder, etc.

    _____

    _____

_____

_____

_____

_____

4.   Determine your labor cost (if necessary). Labor cost should include the cost of contractor support, the cost of your personal effort, and especially the cost of employees' time.

_____

_____

_____

_____

_____

_____

5.   Research if your industry has any wholesale or retail markups. Document what those are!

_____

_____

_____

_____

_____

_____

6.   With the information above, estimate your own cost calculations:

a.   Base Costs = Materials Costs + Labor Costs

_____

_____

_____

_____

_____

_____

b.   Wholesale Costs = (Materials Costs + Labor Costs) x Wholesale Markup

_____

_____

_____

_____

_____

_____

c.   Retail Costs = Wholesale Costs x Retail Markup

_____

_____

_____

_____

d. Profit = (Retail Markup x Items Sold) – Overhead Costs

Let's Recap!

Every year, we watch professional sport's free agents do two things:

1) Price themselves out of their market, or
2) Take less than they're worth.

They need to sit down with their team and come up with a value equivalent to their talent, significance to the team, and market considerations. Like free agents, businesses must ensure they assess their value by considering their product/service offerings, demand, and associated market factors.

TAKEAWAYS:

Play #5

Pay To Win

Financing a business is one of the many reasons why individuals don't follow through with their goals to become self-employed and financially independent. Often it's because the up-front cost is significant enough to persuade them to disregard the future benefits. Many business owners don't plan the financing of their businesses. They have not planned how to turn a dollar spent into two dollars of revenue. It surprises me to hear that many business owners haven't considered all of the necessary equipment, supplies, costs, and services they need to start their businesses.

Every business owner should know exactly what they need and how much they need to open up on day one. Furthermore, business owners should understand how they plan on turning necessary debt financing into revenue and what rate of return are they are willing to accept. Understanding these principles will help business owners address their company's "going-concern", or its ability to operate for one year or more. Again, this goes back to the mistake of preferring execution over planning. However, this is an important piece to get right the first time. You don't simply want to play to win; sometimes you have to pay to win!

Start-up Costs

Businesses are required to spend money before they officially start their operations. Start-up expenses are, by nature, incurred before the business is running. Many people underestimate start-up costs; they either understate what is required to open the business on the first day, or they overestimate the requirements because they have not done the proper research. I don't advise anyone to do this as it makes the start-up process much harder. The best way to adequately measure your start-up costs is to use a start-up worksheet to plan your initial financing. This information is imperative to start initial business account balances relative to the estimated start-up expenses. In some cases, it's better to overestimate, but never underestimate! While you may be able to find some templates with a few Google searches, below are some key areas you should properly document:

➔ Start-up Expenses – These are all of the expenses you will incur in order to open your business for day one operations. For example, many new companies incur legal expenses, graphic design expenses, marketing expenses, branding expenses, physical location expenses, etc.

➔ Start-up Assets – Most often, the only start-up asset a company has is cash (in the form of an established business bank account) or whatever materials related to inventory, systems, or tools needed to start on day one. Other start-up assets, both current and long-term, include equipment, furniture, machinery, etc.

→ Start-up Financing - This includes capital investments and loans. The only investment amounts or loan amounts that should be documented in the start-up worksheet are those that are in the bank on the day you begin operations.

Types of Start-up Financing

An investment is consideration (money or otherwise) that you, or someone else, provides to the company. This is the basic concept of business investments: buying ownership in a company, risking money, or some other consideration in the hopes of attaining a share of the profits later. In today's society, many business owners use debt financing as a way to generate start-up capital. That debt financing is either generated by borrowing from banks, the Small Business Administration, or some other financial means. This also involves using the credit rating of the business owners, which may hinder the amount and the interest rate of the money that can be borrowed. Don't forget about the lesson in persuasion! You can always borrow money from family members or friends that support your vision.

Expect a Loss at Start-up

A degree of loss at start-up is a very common occurrence at this point in the company's life-cycle. In most cases, the business has borrowed more money than the expected yearly profit or the company simply doesn't have sales yet. Again, this is normal. Try not to worry, just start making money.

Cash Balance on Starting Date

A Cash Balance on Starting Date (CBSD) is an estimate of how much money your business needs to have in its checking account when it starts. Your CBSD is the money raised through investments and debt financing minus the cash you need for start-up expenses and start-up assets. When you build your plan for your CBSD, be sure to include a projected cash flow. For example, if your CBSD drops below zero (in your analysis), then you need to increase your projected financing or reduce projected expenses. It's always a good idea to raise enough money to build in contingencies for unexpected expenses or purchases of assets.

Return on Investment (ROI)

The primary purpose of investing in a business venture is to obtain profits. Because investing in a small business is riskier than investing in large corporations, the return on that investment is expected and, in most cases, higher. Most investors use this measure because it can quickly tell them how successful a particular investment in the business can be. Return on investment is used often because it's a very simple measurement to calculate.

The ROI theory is a simple concept. Simply put, a business wants to earn more than one dollar for every dollar spent. Therefore, as long as the ROI calculation is more than 0.00%, it shows that the business is earning more than it is spending or investing. However, the higher the ROI percentage, the more efficiently the business is using its capital. As such, a business should match its ROI to that of other ROIs in the industry to ensure that the company is operating at industry standard. While it is not wise to use ROI as the only means to determine the efficacy of a company, ROI, coupled with other measurements, gives the proper insight into your company's financial health.

Calculating ROI

Depending on its use, an ROI calculation can be extremely complex. For small businesses, it should be relatively simple to avoid making mistakes in the calculation or making decisions based on misinformation. For example, a business owner invests $50,000 in the company and the current year's profit is $10,000. Divide the profit ($10,000) by the total investment ($50,000) to discover that the ROI is 0.20, or 20% for the current year. Small business owners must make sure they use all of their investment amounts to generate an accurate depiction of their company's success. Often smaller amounts are missed, making the ROI percentages inaccurate.

Payback Period

When a small business is trying to decide on a capital expenditure or capital budgeting, it is beneficial to use the payback period as the selection criteria. Small business owners should find it useful to understand the time it takes them to earn back their initial investment in a capital project. This calculation is also effective in estimating cash flows when starting a business. A capital project is usually defined as buying or investing in a fixed asset which will last more than one year. Current projects last less than one year.

The payback period is the number of years it takes to pay back the initial investment of a capital project from the cash flows that the project produces. The capital project could be buying a new operations plant, corporate office space, or new equipment. It is wise to set a cut-off payback period depending on the business, industry, or simply what the owner deems is appropriate. With a cut-off payback period of three years, a company would invest in a capital expenditure if the payback period were 2.5 years, but would pass on a capital expenditure with a payback period of 3.5 years. A business owner should use their own discretion with any calculation using these factors to *inform* their decision, not *make* their decision.

A payback period can be calculated using a simple formula. Payback occurs the year (plus additional months) right before the cash flows turn positive:

$$\text{Payback Period} = \text{Investment Required}/\text{Net Yearly Cash Flow}^*$$
The net yearly cash flow is the amount the investment generates in cash each year.

EXAMPLE: Machine A costs $25,000 and the firm expects payback at the rate of $6,000 per year. Machine B costs $17,000 and the firm expects payback at the same rate as Machine A.

Machine A = $25,000/$6,000 = 4.2 years

Machine B = $17,000/$6,000 = 2.8 years

With all other factors remaining constant, the business owner would select Machine B as they would start making profit somewhere around two years and ten months after purchasing the machine as opposed to four years and two months.

It is important to note that the payback period is not a sure analysis. This calculation does not consider the useful life of each machine, as that would also affect the answer. It also doesn't take into consideration the time value of money, meaning that a dollar today is worth more than a dollar tomorrow. It makes more sense to use the net present value of the cash flows, if that information is available.

Nonetheless, the payback period calculation is a "quick and dirty" method of capital budgeting that can give a business owner a rough estimate of when a capital purchase will pay back their initial investment.

> *"Developing a product or service doesn't mean you have developed a brand."*
>
> — The Marketing Coach

FINANCING EXERCISE:

1. In order to begin your financial research, please complete the following:

    a. Start-up expenses (items that need to be purchased right now):

    _____

    _____

    _____

    _____

    _____

    _____

    b. Start-up assets (capital purchases such as vehicles, office equipment, etc.):

    _____

    _____

    _____

    _____

    _____

    _____

c.   Start-up financing (personal finances, family & friends, angel investors, SBA, etc.):

_____

_____

_____

_____

_____

2.   Using one of the assets listed above:

a.   Research two different versions (cost, enhancements, quality).

_____

_____

_____

_____

_____

b.   Using that information, determine the expected revenue that can be generated per year for each item.

_____

_____

_____

_____

_____

_____

c.   Calculate the payback period of each item using the equation: Cost/Revenue = Payback Period.

_____

_____

_____

_____

_____

_____

3.   What is your expected profit per year? (Be conservative)

_____

_____

_____

_____

_____

_____

4.   What do you plan to invest in your business overall?

_____

_____

_____

_____

_____

_____

5. Using the return-on-investment (ROI) equation of expected profit divided by investment, calculate your expected ROI.

    _____

    _____

    _____

    _____

    _____

    _____

Let's Recap!

Unless baseball is your favorite sport, most major sports organizations have a salary cap. Sports organizations have to ensure they have enough money to put an effective team on the court or on the field to make a run for the championship. In order for businesses to succeed, they need to consider the right mix of financing, whether it is self-funding, taking out a loan, or adding an investor!

TAKEAWAYS:

Play #6

Avoiding Turnovers

E very business owner, at some point, has to keep record of accounting of their financial events. It is imperative to the financial health of a company to keep an accurate record of the expenses and subsequent revenue the company generates. While the latter is important, the overall objective of accounting is to provide external stakeholders (e.g. lenders, creditors, stockholders, etc.) timely, accurate data about the company's financial position. However, before you can start recording business transactions, you must decide whether to use cash-basis or accrual accounting. The crucial difference between these two accounting processes is in how you record your cash transactions.

This section is not intended to be a complete accounting course. There are concepts in this section that will need to be reviewed in detail elsewhere. After this section, please answer the series of questions. While the objective is to answer the questions correctly, it is more important to understand that if you don't know the answer, find it!

Cash-Based Accounting

Cash-based accounting (CBA) is the most commonly used accounting method amongst small business owners because it's the simplest. Based on the size of your business, you may want to start out with CBA, but as your business grows, it may be necessary to switch to accrual accounting in order to more accurately track revenues and expenses.

With CBA, all of the transactions for the reporting period are recorded at the point at which cash actually changes hands. This can be when a cash payment is received by a company from customers or when it is paid by a company for purchases of goods and/or services. The word cash refers to all methods of payment including cash, check, credit card, electronic transfer, or other means commonly used.

You cannot use CBA if you're planning to purchase goods and/or services on account (on credit) or by invoice at a later date. This will force you to set up a liability account referred to as an Accounts Payable account. With CBA, there is no way to record and track money owed to vendors or even money due from customers (Accounts Receivable) at some time in the future using the CBA method.

CBA is good for tracking cash flow, but it is not useful for matching revenues earned with expenses. This becomes most notable when a company buys materials in one month and sells products created by those materials in the following month.

Accrual Accounting

With Accrual Accounting (AA), the major difference from cash basis accounting is that under AA, you record all transactions in your accounting record when they occur, even if you haven't paid them or you haven't been paid. For example, if a customer purchases an item on store credit, the value of the transaction is recorded immediately and an Accounts Receivable balance established until payment is received. Conversely, if you buy goods and/or services on credit, the value of the transaction is entered immediately and an Accounts Payable balance isn't established until payment is made.

Like CBA, AA has its own issues. It adequately matches revenues and expenses but does not adequately track cash. Because you record revenue when you make money and not on the collection of cash, your income statement will show solid revenue generated, even if the money is not in the bank. For example, if you own a contractor-for-hire company, and you complete jobs daily but get paid monthly, you can record the revenue when you complete the job although you haven't collected the cash. If you have slow paying customers, your income statement will show high revenue, but your balance sheet will show low cash.

The Accounting Cycle

As a business owner, it is important to understand the phases of the accounting cycle. Most likely, you may hire someone more competent to perform these tasks; however, it is good business (and required if you're a publicly traded company) to maintain some oversight over the accounting functions of your business. Understanding the basic accounting cycle will get you a step further in having the proper oversight. Keep in mind that you are ultimately responsible for your accounting and tax books, so if your business is audited, they will be asking you questions and not your accountant or accounting firm.

The accounting cycle is never-ending. You start by logging transactions. Those transactions are manipulated through the accounting cycle, and the books close at the end of the accounting period. After that, the entire cycle starts over for the next accounting period. The accounting cycle has eight basic steps, which you can see in the following illustration. The steps are described in the list below.

1. Transactions – Accounting events create financial transactions, which are the start of the process. Transactions can include the sale of a good or service, the purchase of supplies for business activities, or any other financial activity that involves the exchange of the company's assets, the establishment or payoff of a debt, or the deposit from or payout of money to the company's owners.

2. <u>Journal Entries</u> – Journal Entries compile and record the above referenced transactions in the appropriate general ledger account. They follow the basic chart of account entries: Assets (1000), Liabilities/Equity (2000), Revenue (3000), Cost of Goods Sold (4000), Expenses (5000), Memo Accounts (9000). The transaction is listed in the appropriate general ledger account, maintaining the account's chronological order of transactions. The journal is also known as the "book of original entry" because it is where the transaction first appears in a company's accounting system.

3. <u>Posting</u> - The recording of the transactions in the accounts they impact. These accounts are part of the general ledger account mentioned above.

4. <u>Trial Balance</u> - At the end of the accounting period (monthly, quarterly, or yearly depending on a business' practices), you calculate a trial balance. A trial balance is a listing of all of the general ledger accounts contained in the ledger of a business.

5. <u>Worksheet</u> - Unfortunately, many times your first calculation of the trial balance shows that your accounting books aren't in balance. If that's the case, your accounts are reconciled and documented in a worksheet (most likely using MS Excel). The worksheet is also used to calculate the adjustments needed for certain accounts (e.g. the depreciation of assets) and to adjust for one-time payments (such as pre-paid insurance) that will be allocated on a monthly basis to more accurately match monthly expenses with monthly revenues. After you make and record adjustments, you should calculate another trial balance to be sure the accounts are in balance.

6. <u>Adjusting Journal Entries</u> - Once your worksheet shows that your trial balance will be balanced once certain adjustments are recorded to the accounts, you use Adjusting Journal Entries to make a record of the changes. You don't need to make adjusting entries until the trial balance process is completed and all needed corrections and adjustments have been identified.

7. <u>Financial Statements</u> - A document detailing the account balances, incomes, and any other financial information.

8. <u>Closing the Books</u> - You close the books for the revenue and expense accounts and begin the entire cycle again with zero balances in those accounts.

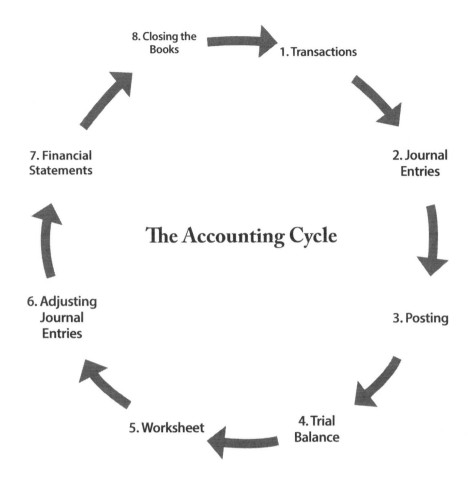

The Accounting Cycle

As a business owner, you want to benchmark and measure your profits or losses on a monthly, quarterly, or yearly basis. In order to do that, your revenue and expense accounts must start with a zero balance at the beginning of each accounting period. Conversely, you carry over asset, liability, and equity account balances from cycle to cycle.

Accounts You Should Never Forget!

Anyone going into business needs to be familiar with the concepts of assets vs. liabilities and revenue vs. expenses. To maintain the life of your business, you should never forget the effect your operations have on its assets, liabilities, revenues, and expenses. Assets and liabilities are the fundamental elements of your company's financial position. Revenue and expenses represent the flow of money through your company's operations.

→ Assets vs. Liabilities - Accounting standards define an asset as something your company owns that can provide future economic benefits. Cash, inventory, accounts receivable, land, buildings, equipment are all assets. Liabilities are your company's obligations — either money that must be paid or services that must be performed. A successful company has more assets than liabilities, meaning it has the resources to fulfill its obligations. On the other hand, a company whose liabilities exceed its assets is probably in trouble.

→ Revenue vs. Expenses - Revenue is money your company earns from conducting business. Expenses are the costs you incur to generate that revenue. That includes the labor, materials, etc. that you need to use to generate the product or service you sell to your customer.

→ Balance Sheet - Your company's assets and liabilities are reported on its balance sheet. Assets go on one side of the sheet, liabilities on the other. The difference between them is the owners' equity in the company (what the owners would take away if they sold all those assets and paid off all those debts). The sheet is "balanced", and must be balanced by definition, when the total value of the company's assets equals the total value of its liabilities plus the total owners' equity.

→ Income Statement - Revenue and expenses appear on your company's income statement. Revenue minus expenses equals your operating profit. Revenue and expenses are distinct from "gains" and "losses," which represent money made or lost on the sale of company assets or other activities outside the day-to-day operations of the company. Gains and losses appear on the income statement separate from revenue and expenses.

Accounting Software & Systems

When starting a business, the last thing you want to worry about is accounting and bookkeeping. Luckily, there are many resources that make performing monthly accounting functions easy. It's best to find an accounting software that is relatively inexpensive and easy to use. This software will keep a record of your most prized possession: your financial position (assets, liabilities, and owner's share). You must also consider cost, ease of use, reporting capabilities, mobile access, service limitations (number of customers, invoices, users, transactions, etc.), customer service, additional services (credit card processing, tax prep, payroll services, etc.), and integration with third-party apps.

The website www.capterra.com lists of some of the most popular accounting software brands currently available. Some of them are listed below. Research each one and make your own determination based on your business' needs:

→ AccountEdge Pro — AccountEdge Pro does more than accounting. It features DIY or outsourced payroll services so you can link accounting to payroll, pay your employees (including direct deposit), track time, and prepare payroll taxes. Retailers also enjoy its inventory management suite, which integrates with popular e-commerce solutions. AccountEdge Pro is available on Mac, Windows, mobile, and in the cloud.

→ FreeAgent — Many accounting software products limit transactions unless you purchase a more expensive package, but FreeAgent offers unlimited users, clients, invoices, expenses, and other functions for one monthly price. It also has a project management feature to help you keep track of billable hours. FreeAgent is best for freelancers, consultants, and other really small business.

→ FreshBooks —FreshBooks offers one of the most user-friendly cloud-based accounting software for non-accountants. It's also a top pick for the best accounting app for iOS and Android devices for offering a wide range of accounting tasks you can perform on the go.

→ GnuCash Free Accounting Software — Is your business powered by Linux? GnuCash is a free, Linux-based accounting software that has all the features small businesses need to manage their finances: income and expense tracking, double-entry accounting, financial reports and calculations, scheduled transactions, and more. It can also track bank accounts, stocks, bonds, and mutual funds.

→ Harvest — Harvest makes it easy to bill clients and get paid. It offers a simple, easy-to-use platform that lets you easily track time and turn billable hours into professional invoices. You can also log expenses, take snapshots and store receipts, generate reports, and connect the app to Google Apps, Salesforce, Basecamp, and more than 50 other business.

→ Hiveage — Need customized accounting software for your freelance or other small business? Unlike your typical accounting platform, Hiveage lets you pick and choose which features to include in your plan, so you only pay for what you need, when you need it.

→ Intacct — Are you a big-picture kind of business owner? Intacct is advanced, cloud-based accounting software that's strictly about business finances and helping your business grow. It can generate a wide range of reports, so you can evaluate your business from any financial angle, including profit margins, losses, income, and revenue segments such as total revenue, revenue by product, revenue by business and revenue histories.

→ Intuit QuickBooks Online — This is my pick for the best accounting software, because Intuit's QuickBooks Online works for all types of small businesses. It offers basic and advanced accounting features, whether you're just starting out, looking to expand, or have been around for some time. Another reason why this is my best pick is because it's mobile. You can update things like mileage, meals, and incidentals on the go. Plus, Intuit software can be uploaded to most online software.

→ Intuit Quicken Home & Business — Quicken, another Intuit accounting product, lets you manage both your personal and business finances in one place. This is perfect for really small businesses and home-based entrepreneurs who don't need a full-blown accounting software designed for more established businesses. The downside, however, is that the software isn't cloud-based.

→ Kashoo — Kashoo's online accounting software can handle your invoices, expense tracking, and double-entry bookkeeping on your computer, smartphone, and tablet. It also offers collaboration features, so you can share your books with your bookkeeper, accountant, investors, and business partners.

→ Less Accounting — Just as its name suggests, Less Accounting helps you spend less time managing your finances and more time running your business. It automates everything from data entry to billing, so you spend minutes instead of hours on your accounting.

→ Outright — Formerly GoDaddy Bookkeeping, Outright simplifies accounting by using bookkeeping data to help you prepare for tax time. It automatically categorizes sales and expenses, and then uses it to prepare your Schedule C, calculate taxes owed, and more.

→ Paychex Accounting Online — Part of the Paychex Payroll Service, Paychex Accounting is a cloud- and mobile-based system that's designed to make accounting easier for you and your accountant. The platform can handle invoices, expenses, reports, and collaboration features to give your accountant, bookkeeper, and other users in order to access to your finances.

➔ Sage One —Sage One has two types of accounting plans: one for invoicing by itself, and another for full-service accounting. The full-service version offers credit card processing and integrates with everything from e-commerce to point-of-sale (POS), customer relationship management (CRM), inventory tracking, document management, and more.

➔ Simple Invoices — If you're a solopreneur and all your accounting needs primarily consist of tracking sales and getting paid, Simple Invoices may be the solution for you. This web app lets you create estimates, send professional invoices, accept payments, generate financial reports and more, absolutely free.

➔ Wave Accounting — Don't want to pay for accounting software? Wave Accounting can help. This web-based accounting platform offers the same features as paid accounting services, making it a top pick for the best free accounting software for small businesses with 10 employees or fewer.

➔ WorkingPoint — WorkingPoint is an all-inclusive accounting software that has everything you need to manage all aspects of your finances: accounting, invoicing, financial reporting, and tax reporting. It's available anytime, anywhere, over the web, or via mobile app.

➔ Xero — Xero is an affordable alternative to QuickBooks Online. Xero is an easy to use, cloud-based accounting software that offers a ton of features and integrates with third-party business solutions you likely already use. It's particularly useful for online stores, as it integrates with 26 e-commerce apps.

➔ Yendo — If you have a lot of customers, multiple businesses, and a dedicated sales team, Yendo is the accounting software for you. It's both an accounting and CRM software, letting you and your sales reps manage and cultivate relationships with customers while linking all the data with your enterprise resource planning and accounting platform.

➔ Zoho Books — Part of the Zoho Office Suite, Zoho Books is a full-featured accounting software with a small business-friendly price tag. Unlike other accounting software that requires more expensive monthly subscriptions for additional features, Zoho Books' comprehensive set of accounting tools is available for one low monthly price.

"Don't compromise your brand for financial gain."

— The Marketing Coach

ACCOUNTING EXERCISE:

Please answer the questions below. As I stated earlier in this chapter, while the objective is to answer the questions correctly, it is more important to understand that if you don't know the answer, find the answer. Perform the necessary research to get the answer. Meet with an accounting professional that can provide the correct answer. It is imperative for every business owner to understand the basic principles of accounting. This concept is referred to as management oversight.

1. Which financial statement presents the revenues and expenses of an organization over an accounting period (e.g. over a month, quarter or year)?

   a. Income Statement.

   b. Balance Sheet.

   c. Cash Flow statement.

   d. Stock Equity Statement.

2. The basic accounting equation includes all of these items EXCEPT:

   a. Assets.

   b. Revenues.

   c. Liabilities.

   d. Stockholder's (Owner's) Equity.

3.   What is the overall purpose of accounting?

   a.   Organize financial transaction data.

   b.   Provide useful information to outside sources about financial position.

   c.   Keep an account of company expenses.

   d.   Reduce tax burden.

4.   In accrual-based accounting, a company's accounting records should be updated for revenues when they are:

   a.   Collected.

   b.   Contracted.

   c.   Earned.

   d.   Readily available.

5.   A _____ is used to record accounting events as they occur throughout the year.

6.   The _____ summarizes the accounting equation in report format. (Note: Ask yourself what is the basic accounting equation.)

7.   Accounts payable is a _____ liability reported on the balance sheet.

8.   On a scale of 1-10, one (1) being novice and ten (10) being expert, what is your level of accounting knowledge? (If you're at the low end, make sure you include accounting services in your start-up budget)

_____

_____

_____

_____

_____

_____

9. If you're currently operating a business, what do you use (software, professional service, self) to perform the necessary accounting functions of your operation?

_____

_____

_____

_____

_____

10. Select an accounting software from the list on the previous pages and answer the following questions:

a. Is it easy to use?

_____

_____

_____

_____

_____

b. What are some things you like about it?

_____

_____

_____

_____

_____

c.   What are some things you dislike about it?

_____

_____

_____

_____

_____

d.   On a scale of 1-10, ten (10) being best, how do you rate the software?

_____

_____

_____

_____

_____

Let's Recap!

Statistics are important to every team and every player because they represent a historical view of the success or failure of the player or team. Sports organizations use these statistics to make decisions on the performance of teams and players to assess their value and productivity. Accounting is the cornerstone of every company as it is necessary to assess the performance and productivity of the prospective organization!

TAKEAWAYS:

3rd Quarter

Play #7

Business Viability: Would You Buy Your Own Product?

Everyone buys things and everyone has opinions on where they like to buy, how they like to buy, and what makes them buy. Small business owners/entrepreneurs seem to forget these experiences when they plan to enter their product or service into the market. Take the time to consider the reasons your prospective customers have for making personal decisions on spending before you develop the product, the marketing, and the branding that will display this product to the masses.

There are many reasons people buy things. Even though you are an entrepreneur, you're bound to align with one of these two major reasons: reputation or quality.

Product or Manufacturer Reputation

Know the importance of brand recognition. What guides a product's reputation? Experiences! When enough people have had a great experience with your product or service, it develops a reputation, which then develops the brand. If a company's reputation is respectable in terms of the product or service it sells (i.e. consumer electronics), customers are willing to pay a premium for the name. Keep in mind that reputations go both ways; products can be considered first-class or last-class.

Consumers are flooded with advertising every day, which makes it easier for advertising to be ignored. If you think about it, a start-up could simply create a fancy website, develop some business cards, a basic advertising strategy, and blend in with every other company out there. That's why it's important for your brand to deliver the big win and not just talk about how to win. In reality, brand position is owned, not bought. How does a company earn its brand position? It earns that position by following through on the developing of the brand reputation through quality products and services.

Quality

The only way a company can survive in today's industries is by earning full customer satisfaction. You must deliver high quality products or services constantly and consistently. Quality can be defined in a number of ways, but today the ultimate measure of quality is achieving customer satisfaction. The definition of high quality products and services has to be flexible, as customer needs change overtime and are affected by what your competitors offer. In short, there could be a "need" in the industry today that may not be there tomorrow.

Another way to define quality is excellence. Excellence is not perfection, but it simply means your business is doing everything it needs to do daily to deliver a winning product or service. The goal should always be to deliver the product or service without issue or error.

"How then, do you build quality in your company?" Good question! There are many different quality management structures that a company can follow to exhibit the highest quality, for example, Six Sigma, DMAIC, and others. To make this easy, if a company follows these five building blocks, it will be able to build excellence in quality:

➜   Continuous improvement philosophy.

➜   Consistency in everything you do.

➜   Teamwork as part of the culture.

➜   Routine measurement and analysis.

➜   Training for all.

Continuous Improvement is simply implementing constant checks and balances in the organization to note where improvements can be implemented. As quality and productivity improve, costs are reduced, and customer satisfaction increases. These combined effects produce a double benefit to an organization's profit margin. Companies that consistently monitor their business practices and their costs, and improve where necessary, often do well in terms of profitability.

Consistency is one of the significant elements for *continuous improvement*. No matter the type of business you have, it should be your goal to perform every function within the organization the same way every time. Standardization is necessary in any company as long as it doesn't inhibit innovation, as you need both to grow and prosper in your business.

Teamwork is an essential part of doing business these days. Teamwork makes the dream work! A team approach should be deep-rooted in your company's culture so that every person understands how they contribute to the greater good of the organization as a whole.

Measurement and analysis of your operations and your enterprise will help you better understand what's working well and what needs improvement in your business operations. Set benchmarks in service, delivery, or your product, so that you can review after a period of performance to see if you're meeting your objectives, surpassing the benchmark, or not meeting your company's performance goals. This is paramount to the effectiveness of any organization and necessary to continually improve.

Training and education are the most significant building blocks for quality. How can your organization run smoothly if no one knows what they're doing? Maybe you have a niche industry with specific requirements. Well, employees need to be trained so that they can perform the other four building blocks to quality. To make all of the building blocks to quality work in unison, the members of your organization need to understand what you're trying to accomplish. They need to know your mission, understand your goals, and understand the importance of meeting the company's benchmarks. Training is the only way your organization will operate competently, efficiently, and consistently on a daily basis.

"Employees that believe in your brand become advocates for it."

— The Marketing Coach

BRAND REPUTATION EXERCISE:

Answer each question whether you have the answer or not. It is best to document these answers so that you'll know the areas in which your organization needs to improve.

1. What training can you use to help your team understand the importance of quality?

_____

_____

_____

_____

_____

_____

2.   What can you do to improve the quality of your product or service?

_____

_____

_____

_____

_____

_____

3.   Do you have a method to measure and analyze your product and your operations?

_____

_____

_____

_____

_____

_____

4.   After the initial analysis, did you discover an issue with your product or service? What was your issue?

_____

_____

_____

Let's Recap!

Many professional athletes would probably have been more successful in sports had they not ruined their reputations or damaged their bodies outside of their respective sport. Names abound, but they will not be mentioned here! What business owners should learn from the examples of these athletes is that product, service quality, and reputation are paramount! Get either of these three things wrong and your business will have nothing to offer!

TAKEAWAYS:

Play #8

You Win As A Team, You Lose As A Team

There are many challenges that business owners face when starting a company. One major challenge is the human resources side of the business. Boundless.com defines human resources as "the set of individuals who make up the workforce of an organization, business sector, or an economy." The professional discipline and business function that oversees an organization's human resources is called human resource management (HRM, or simply HR). No matter if your business is big or small, all parts of human resources are the same and all companies need to use HR techniques.

Many of the questions involved in starting a business revolve around human resources. How many people should you hire? What tasks can you do yourself vs. hiring someone to do them? What positions are necessary and what positions can wait? Do you need to offer benefits and if so, what benefits? Do you need someone to handle payroll? Who can write employee reviews and be in charge of training? All these questions are part of human resources. To have a functional successful business, you must take care of your employees. The way to do this is to know about and utilize human resources.

So as a small business owner you may ask, *"What should I focus on the most? Are there any major challenges that I may face because of an improper HR system?"* Well I am glad you asked! As a small business owner, the focus should be hiring the right staff. Because you are a small business owner, it is very important to hire the right people for the right positions. This is important because every position is key and it takes a lot of time and money to hire someone. Without the right people in place, it is difficult to get things done. It also hinders your business and holds you back. Hiring the right person can be very difficult. The first step is identifying what skills and characteristics a person must have in order to do the job properly. Hold true to what you want — the right person is out there. You might have to pay more in some cases, but it is worth it if it is the right person. Some people interview well but have no work ethic. You can never be 100% sure you have hired the right person. Hiring is definitely a game of chance, but taking the right steps can take some of the chance out of it. The type of interview questions you ask is one way to help you secure the right candidate.

The best type of questions are behavior-based interview questions. Below are examples of behavior-based questions:

→ *Talk about a time when you had several tasks to get done that were all due at the same time.*

→ *Tell me how you prioritized them, what the outcome was, and what would you change next time.*

By asking behavior-based questions, it forces the applicant to show creativity and comprehension. It also shows you a person's work ethic and style of work. If the person has never had several tasks to do at once, then odds are they might have never had a real job before or the candidate may have no sense of urgency.

Sourcing

Finding good talent is called sourcing. In human resources, there are two types of sourcing:

➜ Passive Sourcing – Identifying a candidate that would be a good fit but they are presently employed and not really looking for a new job.

➜ Direct Sourcing – Looking for a candidate that would be a good fit that is looking for a new opportunity.

There are many different avenues that are helpful for sourcing candidates: LinkedIn Recruiter, CareerBuilder, and Indeed, just to name a few. Each source has an applicant side and an employer side. For a fee, you can post your open jobs to these sites, as well as go through their databases of applicants. LinkedIn Recruiter is a great way to find passive candidates. On LinkedIn Recruiter, you can read profiles, check work experience, see a picture of the potential candidate, and send the candidate a direct message to their profile.

HUMAN RESOURCES EXERCISE:

Below are some questions to ask yourself when you feel you need to hire someone to help run your business.

1. What is your recruiting budget?

_____

_____

_____

_____

_____

_____

2.   How much are you willing to spend to get the right person?

_____

_____

_____

_____

_____

3.   How much time can you devote per day to sourcing? If you do not want to hire someone to do the sourcing for you, can you do it yourself?

_____

_____

_____

_____

_____

4.   Who will bring this person up to speed on the job?

_____

_____

_____

_____

_____

5.   Do you have time to train?

_____

_____

_____

_____

_____

6.   Are you able to complete your goals each day?   (If you're not completing your tasks in a timely fashion, you made need some help)

_____

_____

_____

_____

_____

Sourcing is very time consuming and takes patience and determination. Answering the few questions above will let you know if you need to hire additional employees and if you can hire someone to assist you with acquiring talent. Recruiting good talent is a full-time job and can be stressful to someone who has never done it before, so don't be too hard on yourself!

Job Description

When using these databases to find talent, you must first write a good job description for the positions you need filled. Your job description will help you attract the right candidate. Naming the skills needed for the job is very important. Here are the critical pieces that must be included in a job description:

→ Job title

→ Job description

→ Company mission statement

→ Qualifications

→ Special skills or demands

→ Job duties and responsibilities

Always remember to add "other duties as assigned" in your description. You want to hire someone who will jump in and help in any way they can. Most employers like to think all employees are this way. That is incorrect — most people stick to the job description. Adding a simple disclaimer like "other job duties as assigned" will cover the grey area and keep you from hearing them say, "That's not in my job description." It is also nice to include a salary range. Having a salary range listed in your job description will eliminate people who don't want to work for what you are offering. When looking at talent, you want to make sure the individual you are considering buys into your company! The more they believe in what your company is doing and what it stands for, the better your employee will do and ultimately, the better your company will do. You are only as good as the people who work for you.

JOB DESCRIPTION EXERCISE:

1. Name the position you need filled:

    _____

2. What is your company's mission statement?

    _____

_____
_____
_____
_____
_____

3.   What do you need that person to do?

_____
_____
_____

4.   What skills are needed to be able to get the job done correctly?

_____
_____
_____

5.   What type of personality works best with your team and gets things done correctly?

_____
_____
_____
_____
_____
_____

6.   Do research on salary requirements for the positions you need and determine a proper salary range for those positions (research your industry and geographic area).

_____

_____

_____

_____

_____

POTENTIAL EMPLOYEES EXERCISE:

Below is a checklist of questions that can help you with potential employees. Answer accordingly.

☐   Describe your current need for an employee (if you feel there are not enough hours in a day, you might need assistance).

_____

_____

_____

_____

_____

☐   How will you preform background checks and reference checks?

_____

_____

_____

_____

_____

_____

☐ What will be this employee's salary? (Always know the market price, and if you cannot afford to pay it, have other values that will keep your employee happy.)

_____

_____

_____

_____

☐ What are individuals being paid in this position in your industry and geographic area?

_____

_____

_____

_____

☐ Do you need a payroll system? If so, which one will you use?

_____

_____

_____

_____

_____

_____

☐ How many employees do you currently have?

_____

_____

_____

_____

_____

☐ Will you offer benefits to your employees?

_____

_____

_____

_____

_____

Payroll

Paying your employees on time and correctly is very important. There is nothing worse than trying to get work out of someone who has not been paid correctly and on time. There are a few payroll systems that can assist with this. Major ones are APD, Kronose, and QuickBooks. Also, companies that have 50 or more full-time employees are required by the government to offer health insurance for employees. Make sure to shop around for benefits and remember that employees always have the option to go on their own with benefits. American Family and Aetna are a couple of places to start.

Training and Development

Once you have the employee on board, orientation is very important for the employee to learn everything about your company from culture, what your company stands for, and how to perform their job duties properly. Do not just throw the employee a tremendous amount of work and expect them to deliver. You must take the time to train the individual efficiently. The best way to go about this is to have a standard training system in place. Each employee should be considered "in training" and on probation for at least 90 days. By making this clear in orientation, if you have made a bad hire, you will be able to tell within those first 90 days. Hands-on training should last at least two weeks. Easing the employee into the role will allow for fewer mistakes down the road. Also, be sure to check to see if your state is an "at-will" state. An "at-will" state is a state where you can terminate employment for any reason at any time without just cause and the employee can quit for any reason at any time without just cause.

When doing employee training, you have two options: 1) You can have someone who is in the position, and excels at it, train the new employee, or 2) You can hire a person for training and development. Whichever you decide, keep in mind that the employee will do things the way the trainer teaches them and it is hard to break any bad habits. On the following page, you will see an example of a simple training guide. It is very important to keep documentation on everything you do. Also, you want to be sure you are teaching each person the same thing. In human resources, it is very important to be consistent, fair, and to have documentation for everything.

Training and Development

Title: Customer Service Training Guide

Employee:

Effective Dates:

Training	Completed Date	Trainer's Name	Pass/ Fail	Employee Signature/ Trainee Signature
Orientation				
Completed Paperwork				
Cashier Training				
Customer Service Training				
Return Policy				
Service Desk				
Closing				
Cross Training				

"You cannot be innovative with a disengaged staff."

— The Marketing Coach

Let's Recap!

Sometimes it takes sports organizations years to find the right pieces to a championship puzzle. The right key pieces have to fit together in order to form the team that the organization wants. Talent costs, so do not have the mindset of cutting corners or trying to get someone for cheap. At the end of the day, you get what you pay for. If key players are needed in certain positions, you have to pay.

There are other creative ways to fill important positions that are added bonuses at the time, such as internships, volunteer opportunities, or even work study programs, so do not be afraid to explore all of your options. Starting a business is a lot of hard work, so it will take dedication from yourself and anyone else who you decide to take on this journey. You now have the tools that are necessary to win in this sport we call business, so go out, be great, and build that dynamic team!

TAKEAWAYS:

Play #9

The Market

The number one thing that I tell my clients is that you have to build a brand before you can even think about marketing to any type of consumer. This is a concept that I like to call *Brand before Market*, which means no matter how long it takes, you need to put in the time to develop your brand. Nurture your brand so that when it's ready to go to market, you will make that desired connection between your brand and your consumer. Your brand exists to tell a story about what your intellectual property (e.g. company, trade, product, service) stands for and the audience it serves. You can discover the effectiveness of your branding by asking yourself the following questions:

1. *"Is the brand that I have created up to this point, the brand that I want the world to know?*

2. *"Did I make the mistake of marketing before branding?"*

I define marketing as gaining the attention of your target client through strategies that relay your brand's message. The biggest piece to marketing that has to come first is identifying who your target market is. This is something that we reviewed previously while doing your brand research. You only have one chance to make a first impression, so do not start promoting or marketing your brand or business until you are truly ready to go to market. By no means am I saying that everything will be perfect or that you will have everything you need, but based on your industry and what we covered in the previous plays, you will be at a great starting point if you follow the steps that are provided. Once you have identified who your client is, then based on your product or service, a proper strategy can be implemented to reach them. There is no cookie cutter answer when it comes to defining what your marketing strategy is going to be.

The goals of your marketing strategies should be to build brand awareness, increase customer engagement, and establish brand loyalty to help further the success of your organization. Marketing is forever changing because the world is forever changing. Technology has made it easier to reach consumers, but it has also made it harder because the attention span is so short now in our digital world. Keeping up with the latest trends and opportunities to get your business in front of the consumer is important for your brand, but you cannot solely rely on marketing to keep your business thriving. Focusing on customer service is essential because word travels fast, especially if it's bad news. People spread bad experiences faster than they spread good ones. Now with technology, it is easier to share this information with the world because everything is right at our fingertips.

When you start to market your business, understand that content is key and the one who produces the most content stays ahead of the curve. You want to always be creating content, whether it's digital, print, videos, or blogs in order to keep your consumer engaged with your product at all times. Based on your industry, you will have a better feel of what that looks like. For example, if I have a clothing brand, then I want to push my product with as much content as possible. That means coming up with sales, display boards for new products, photo shoots of the latest releases, or commercials if budgets permit. You should have a team of people that is constantly coming up with ideas and ways to push your product to your consumer based on their likes and dislikes, which you learn through completing your brand research. The more you produce content and analyze the data and feedback you receive, the better you will know what your customer responds to.

Market Research

Research your direct competitors. Why should people buy your product or service over your competitor's? It is important to know what products or services exist in the industry that you are trying to enter. There is nothing wrong with studying their moves to see what's working for them and what's not working for them. You have to be creative in developing your own voice and niche, but in order to be a strong competitor, you must see what you're up against so that you're not going into the business blind to industry standards. In certain cases, you don't want to overprice yourself out of the game or even under value your business.

With launching the brand of The Marketing Coach, it was a strategic move by my team, The Boyd Group. I was the first client of the company because we wanted to take people on the journey with us as we openly developed my brand in the eyes of the public. My vision was for people to see how to really develop a brand and how long it actually takes. Think about a professional basketball player who, on average, enters the league at the age of 20 and has been putting in work to get there, in some cases, for 15 years. They put in countless amounts of hours and years to achieve their goals of being one of the best in the game. This is the approach that I took when I finally decided to help people and businesses with their brands and strategies. After all the years I put in working for other people and getting two degrees in business and marketing, I felt that I was ready. I researched great people in the industry and studied what they have done to get to this point. I had to figure out what would separate me from everyone else but at the same time stay true to my voice. I used my life experience of sports combined with the knowledge of marketing and branding in order to come up with the brand I have today, which is The Marketing Coach with the tagline, 'Marketing is My Sport'.

Research your indirect competitors. Once you have identified your target audience, I encourage you to find some indirect competitors. These are companies that are selling a different product or service but have the same clientele. This strategy comes in handy when you're developing your marketing strategies because it allows you to study their behaviors when it comes to buying products or using particular services.

Research your employees. This is very important. Your employees are people you can trust and who can deliver your brand's message. You want to make sure that you hire someone to handle the onboarding process of new employees so that they are properly trained and have a clear understanding of what the mission and vision is of the company. Having a strong interview process is imperative because you want to make sure that you can learn as much about a person as you can before giving them a job with your company or hiring them to represent your brand, which we discussed in Play #8.

Research your customers. Research the likes and dislikes of your customers, their emotions, and what makes them buy products. Take this a step further and create a client profile. This will help you know exactly who this person is so that when it's time to market your product, you know who you are talking to. You need to make sure that your brand's message is clear. The way you do that is by developing a strong understanding of your audience. Below is an exercise that you can do to pinpoint the individuals who will most likely buy your product. This exercise will not be the determining factor because you may have to revisit this from time to time after your product or service goes to market and you get data that shows who is actually buying your product or using your services.

PROSPECT PROFILE EXERCISE:

1. What is the age range of your customer?

    _____

    _____

2. What is the problem he or she is having?

    _____

    _____

3. How does your company or brand solve that problem?

    _____

    _____

4. What are their hobbies and interest?

    _____

5. Are they a business or an individual?

6. Where is this kind of clientele located?

7. What are their beliefs?

8. What do they need from you?

9. What stores do they frequent?

10. Where do they hang out?

11. What do they read?

12.　Who are they following?

_____

_____

13.　How can you connect with their network?

_____

_____

14.　How much disposable income do they have?

_____

_____

15.　Are they employed?

_____

_____

16.　What is their relationship status?

_____

_____

17.　Do they have children?

_____

_____

18.　What is their education level?

_____

_____

19.   What is their income level?

_____

_____

20.   Are they entrepreneurs? If so, where are they in their business?

_____

_____

21.   How many times a year do they buy the kind of product/service your company provides?

_____

_____

22.   How much does he or she spend on your products or services in a year?

_____

_____

23.   What benefit will they gain from your brand and product?

_____

_____

MEET YOUR PROSPECT EXERCISE:

Write a detailed scouting report of your ideal prospect based on all the questions you answered above. Give this prospect a name and write who they are to your brand.

_____

_____

_____

_____

_____

_____

Marketing Strategies

Traditional marketing uses a more in-person approach to getting your message and brand to your audience. Although it can be more time consuming, it is a great way to build personal relationships with your customers. Digital marketing, on the other hand, is the marketing of your product or service through different forms of electronic media. Today's consumers spend a lot of time on their electronic devices, so it is important that you get your brand in front of them. What better way to do this than to speak to them on these devices? The following are descriptions of different traditional and digital marketing tactics:

→ Guerrilla Marketing - Innovative, unconventional, and low-cost marketing techniques aimed at obtaining maximum exposure for a product. For example, hitting the streets and canvasing the neighborhood or communities with your product. This can be done several different ways: you can do hand-to-hand flyers or business cards, putting up posters, placing information on cars and in businesses, or community boards at the library and city halls. But the thing you want to keep in mind is that you want to choose one of these that falls best in line with your brand.

→ Business Cards - A small card printed with your name, professional occupation, company position, business address, and other contact information. When networking and meeting new people, it is imperative that you always hand out your card when making connections while taking business cards from other people that you are networking with.

→ Flyers - A piece of marketing collateral that is handed out to promote, advertise, or market a particular event or product. Digital flyers have become the newest alternative and are mostly effective on social media.

→ Website – This is your home base for information on the internet. The majority of your potential clients will visit your website first to learn more about what you offer. Always make sure that your site is up to the highest standard.

→ Direct Mail - A marketing effort that uses a mail service to deliver a promotional printed piece to your target audience. I know that this may seem like junk mail that people throw away, but this technique is still useful when it is done the right way. With this, you still have to be creative in your approach because you want the mailer to stick out and entice someone to open it.

→ Billboards - A large outdoor board or sign for displaying advertisements. You usually see these in some neighborhoods on your main streets, around businesses, as well as along the highways and interstates. Billboards drive great impressions, which refers to the number of times someone is seeing your advertisement.

→ Coupons - Offering a coupon is a great way to introduce people to your product. Making them feel as though they are getting a deal is a great way to make a connection with that consumer.

→ Merchandise - Branded promotional items or products, which are used in marketing campaigns or giveaways to raise company awareness. These are good for giveaways at different events such as trade shows and festivals, and they give your brand legs because your messaging is in the hands of potential clients.

→ Media-TV/Radio - Outlets that are used to advertise events or products to the masses. TV and radio commercials usually vary in price depending on the content as well as the length of the ad.

→ Search Engine Optimization (SEO) – This is a marketing strategy used to increase visits to your website. This is done with your website developers. It involves listing key words on your site that allow you to be organically ranked higher when they are searched on search engines. You want to pay attention to this when adding content to your site. Make sure that you're using content and key words that your consumer is looking for when they are searching for similar product or services.

→ Email Marketing – This is a very cost effective way to connect with consumers that have shown an interest in your brand by subscribing to your website. Use this platform and create personalized messages for your leads, consumers, and target audience. There are free services like Mail Chimp that can make your email marketing efforts easier and user friendly.

➔ <u>Pay Per Click Advertising</u> – This is the best method to use when you want to give maximum website visibility to those consumers who are searching for your business or similar ones on search engines. A pay-per-click system is used for paid listings in which the advertiser pays for each click on their ad. This is also great if you're running a special and you want to buy ads through Google AdWords, Bing Ads, or Yahoo advertising.

➔ <u>Website Display Advertising</u> – This method is done by displaying ads on various websites in different formats such as video, text, or images. This is a great way to raise awareness about your brand. You want to make sure that your ads are very engaging and that they drive people to click on those ads, which should lead them to your website or landing page. If you're tying this into a campaign, then you can even get specific about who you want to reach—targeting websites that your customer may frequent at the ideal time of day, location, gender, etc.

➔ <u>Retargeting Advertising</u> – This is a method of advertising that is used to stain the image of your brand in your audience's mind. Retargeting uses advertisements to target users who have previously visited your website in the past. This makes the consumer familiar with your brand and encourages them to purchase whichever item they were looking at on your site.

➔ <u>Video Marketing</u> – Make sure that you are using videos to tell your brand's story and create captivating videos that bring your story to life so that you can engage your audience. With the internet being such a powerful tool, great videos and stories can be shared all over the world to make a connection with your potential client. You want to be constantly sharing your videos via your social media pages, website, and YouTube channel.

Brand Positioning

"What is your position in the market — the place that is exclusively yours?"

"Do you walk or talk like anyone else in your market or industry?"

When thinking about these questions, I want you to think about what makes your brand unique, what makes your product or service unique, and what is unique about working for your company/ organization. Digging a little deeper, I want you to identify what void you are filling in the market, or why people are going to buy what you are selling. This does not mean that you always have to reinvent the wheel by coming out with a product that is not on the market, but you may have a great idea that may enhance an existing product or service, as long as it's unique and not being done anywhere else.

The key to all of this is your customer experience. In a digital world where consumers have a short attention span, focusing on your brand experience is paramount because this is what gives you your competitive advantage. But before you can identify your position in the market, you have to identify your target market or audience.

NICHE EXERCISE:

Answer the following questions to identify your niche - that place that is only yours in the market:

1. Who are you selling to?

_____

_____

2. Who is buying your product?

_____

_____

3. Who is in need of your service?

_____

_____

4. Why do they need your service?

_____

_____

5. What is your competitive advantage?

_____

_____

6.   How are you differentiating yourself from the competition?

_____

_____

7.   What is the latest behavior of your target market?

_____

_____

8.   How visually appealing are your marketing materials? How can you improve them?

_____

_____

9.   What is the overall feeling that your marketing materials portray?

_____

_____

10.   How up-to-date are your marketing materials in terms of content?

_____

_____

11.   Is the website functional, easy to navigate, and updated?

_____

_____

12.   Are people talking about your company via word of mouth?

> "Your customer experience will be your competitive advantage. Your customer experience will outweigh your prices."
>
> — The Marketing Coach

CUSTOMER EXPERIENCE EXERCISE:

Put yourself in the shoes of the client/customer.

1. In this section describe, if you're already in business, what your customers are currently experiencing with your brand?

_____

_____

_____

_____

_____

_____

2. Describe what you would like your customers to experience with this brand or company within the next 12 months.

_____

_____

_____

_____

_____

_____

3. What is your plan to get to your desired experience for your client?

_____

_____

_____

_____

_____

_____

"Marketing wins clients. Branding wins contracts."

— The Marketing Coach

Let's Recap!

Now let's remember that our clients and customers are the most important pieces when it comes to marketing our brands, products, and services. In today's world of business, customer experience is the new marketing; they can make or break your business, so you have to always be mindful of them in whatever you do. Treat every transaction with care and listen to all feedback whether good or bad because it allows you to make adjustments along the way. There are a lot of strategies discussed in this chapter and I do not want you to be intimidated by trying to figure out what is going to work for your business or brand. Make sure you do your research for your industry and go from there when making your selection process!

TAKEAWAYS:

4th Quarter

Play #10

A-Game: Time To Execute

I am so excited that you are ready to start your business! You have trained, worked, and now it's time to hit this playing field we call life and introduce this well-oiled, branded business to the world! It is important that you take your time and remember all the details we discussed in this playbook because it will be vital to the success of your business. We covered a lot of key factors through the many plays in this playbook and you have to remember that you want to brand your business before marketing. Skipping steps is not an option and I want you to take the time to do it right because you owe it to yourself to go through the entire branding process in order to give your business its greatest chance to reach the highest potential in your industry. Be sure to find the right people, no matter how long it takes, because your employees become your brand advocates in a good way as well as a bad way. We touched a lot on human resource management, so do not hesitate to hire someone to handle this for you because we know how important this is to your business.

Just think, the hard part is over! You have done all the necessary preparation and now it's time to face your fear and actually get started running and operating your business! This is the time to get excited and pump your team up on this new adventure! I want you to inspire your team to be the best that they can be because you want to take over your industry and dominate the market. To do that, your team has to understand the task at hand and become warriors for the brand. Do not think that you won't face any road blocks or adversity along this journey. I am confident that after going through this material, you will be better prepared to handle anything thrown your way! Do not run from any problems that you face in your business. Take it head on because you are ready and you have developed a strong foundation!

The number one thing that I encourage you to take from this experience is that your customers are everything and they drive everything that you do. Customer experience is the new marketing, so don't allow this aspect of your business to fall by the wayside because you're busy focusing on other aspects of the business. I'm not saying that things surrounding your business operations are not important, but your customer's opinions, experiences, like and dislikes, should be at the top of your list because this is what will make them loyal to your brand.

I would like to thank you for allowing me to be your coach in this game we call business.
I am Donovan Boyd, The Marketing Coach, and Marketing Is My Sport.

Words To Remember

401(K) Plan: A qualified employer-established plan to which eligible employees may make salary deferral (salary reduction) contributions on a post-tax and/or pre-tax basis.

Background Check: The act of reviewing both confidential and public information to investigate a person or entity's history.

Base Wage: The initial rate of compensation an employee receives in exchange for services.

Behavioral Interview: A job interviewing technique whereby the applicant is asked to describe past behavior in order to determine whether he or she is suitable for a position.

Benefits: In-direct and non-cash compensation paid to an employee.

Brand Loyalty: The extent of the faithfulness of consumers to a particular brand. Brand loyalty is expressed through their repeat purchases, despite the marketing pressure generated by the competing brands.

Brand Management: A function of marketing that uses techniques to increase the perceived value of a product line or brand over time. Effective brand management enables the price of products to go up and builds loyal customers through positive brand associations, images, or a strong awareness of the brand.

Breakeven Point: Point in time (or in number of units sold) when forecasted revenue exactly equals the estimated total costs; where loss ends and profit begins to accumulate. This is the point at which a business, product, or project becomes financially viable.

Business Loan: Borrowed capital that companies apply toward expenses that they are unable to pay for themselves.

Business Plan: A written document that describes in detail how a new business is going to achieve its goals. A business plan will lay out a written plan from a marketing, financial, and operational viewpoint.

Confidentially Agreement: A legal agreement between two or more parties that is used to signify that a confidential relationship exists between the parties.

Copyright: The ownership of intellectual property by the item's creator.

Cross Branding: A marketing strategy which combines two offerings from separate companies. The technique is usually used to sell complementary products or services.

Customer Service: The assistance and advice provided by a company to those people who buy or use its products or services. Customer service is an extremely important part of maintaining ongoing client relationships, which are key to continuing revenue.

Digital Marketing: A subcategory of marketing that uses digital technology to place and sell products.

Entrepreneur: An individual who, rather than working as an employee, runs a small business and assumes all the risks and rewards of a given business venture, idea, or good/service offered for sale.

Going Concern: The ability for an organization to function without the threat or risk of dissolution for an entire year. A company's "going concern" or functionality is assessed every year.

Guerrilla Marketing: A marketing tactic in which a company uses surprise and/or unconventional interactions in order to promote a product or service. Guerrilla marketing is different than traditional marketing in that it often relies on personal interaction, has a smaller budget, and focuses on smaller groups of promoters that are responsible for getting the word out in a particular location rather than on wide-spread media campaigns.

Human Resources (HR): The company department charged with finding, screening, recruiting, training job applicants, as well as administering employee-benefit programs.

Income Statement: A financial statement that measures a company's financial performance over a specific accounting period.

Internship: A temporary position with an emphasis on on-the-job training rather than merely employment. This can be paid or unpaid.

Inventory: The raw materials, work-in-process products, and finished goods that are considered to be the portion of a business' assets that are ready or will be ready for sale.

Investor: Any person who commits capital with the expectation of financial returns.

Job Description: The description of the responsibilities associated with a given job.

Limited Liability Company (LLC): A corporate structure whereby the members of the company cannot be held personally liable for the company's debts or liabilities. Limited liability companies are essentially hybrid entities that combine the characteristics of a corporation and a partnership or sole proprietorship.

Limited Liability Partnership (LLP): A business organization that allows limited partners to enjoy limited personal liability while general partners have unlimited personal liability.

Marketing Strategy: An organization's strategy that combines all of its marketing goals into one comprehensive plan. A good marketing strategy should be drawn from market research, focus on the right product mix in order to achieve the maximum profit potential, and should sustain the business.

Networking: Creating a group of acquaintances/associates and keeping it active through regular communication for mutual benefit. Networking is based on the question *"How can I help?"* versus *"What can I get?"*

Non-Compete Agreement: An agreement between two parties, typically an employee and employer, by which the employee agrees not to use information learned during employment in subsequent business efforts for a set period of time.

Organizational Chart: A diagram that outlines the internal structure of a company. An organizational chart is the most common visual depiction of how an organization is structured. It outlines the roles, responsibilities, and relationships between individuals within an organization. An organizational chart can be used to depict the structure of an organization as a whole, or broken down by department or unit.

Product Development: The overall process of strategy, organization, concept generation, product creation, marketing plan evaluation, and commercialization of a new product.

Profit and Loss Statement (P&L): A financial statement that summarizes the revenues, costs, and expenses incurred during a specific period of time; usually a fiscal quarter or year.

Recruiting: The process of finding and hiring the best-qualified candidate (from within or outside of an organization) for a job opening, in a timely and cost-effective manner.

Retirement: The act of leaving one's business or occupation and no longer working.

Solopreneur: An entrepreneur who works alone, "solo," running their business single-handedly. They might have contractors for hire, yet have full responsibility for the running of their business.

Standard Operating Procedure (SOP): Written instructions intended to document how to perform a routine activity. Many companies rely on standard operating procedures to help ensure consistency and quality in their products.

Terms of Employment: The conditions that an employer and employee agree upon for a job. Terms of employment include an employee's job responsibilities, work days, hours, breaks, dress code, vacation, sick days, and pay. They also include benefits such as health insurance, life insurance, and retirement plans.

Trademark: A recognizable insignia, phrase, or other symbol that denotes a specific product or service and legally differentiates it from all other products.

Training and Development: The official and ongoing educational activities within an organization designed to enhance the fulfillment and performance of employees.

Start-up Checklist:

- ☐ Accountant/ Accounting software
- ☐ Articles of Incorporation
- ☐ Brand Colors
- ☐ Business Account
- ☐ Business Cards
- ☐ Business Plan
- ☐ Business Trademark
- ☐ Business/Federal Licenses
- ☐ Competitors
- ☐ Content Creator
- ☐ Core Values
- ☐ Domain Name
- ☐ Graphic Designer

- ☐ Growth Strategy
- ☐ Hashtags
- ☐ Hiring Procedure
- ☐ Labor Costs
- ☐ Location
- ☐ Logo
- ☐ Marketing Strategy
- ☐ Material Costs
- ☐ Mission Statement
- ☐ Non-competitors
- ☐ Organizational Structure
- ☐ Overhead Cost
- ☐ Payback Period
- ☐ Payroll System

- ☐ Potential Employees
- ☐ Product Manufacturer
- ☐ Profit Margin
- ☐ Recruiting Budget
- ☐ Social Media Pages
- ☐ Standard Operating Procedures
- ☐ Starting Date
- ☐ Tagline
- ☐ Target Market
- ☐ Tax Identification Number
- ☐ Vision Statement
- ☐ Uniforms
- ☐ Web Developer
- ☐ Webpage

Appendices & Resource Section

1. "Brand." Webster Dictionary: The New American. New York: New American Library, 1958. Print.

2. "U.S. Small Business Administration | The U.S. Small Business Administration | SBA.gov." U.S. Small Business Administration | The U.S. Small Business Administration | SBA.gov. N.p., n.d. Web. 28 July 2016.

3. "Consumer Affairs." NIKE, Inc. N.p., n.d. Web. 28 July 2016.

4. "Company – Google." Company – Google. N.p., n.d. Web. 28 July 2016.

5. "Mission and Values." NFL. N.p., n.d. Web. 28 July 2016.

6. "Our Mission." Special Olympics. N.p., n.d. Web. 28 July 2016.

7. "Mission, Vision & Values." Mission, Vision & Values. N.p., n.d. Web. 28 July 2016.

8. "I Just Used Capterra to Find Software!" Software: Business & Nonprofit. N.p., n.d. Web. 28 July 2016.

9. "Business Credit - Business Credit for Small Business." Business Credit. N.p., n.d. Web. 28 July 2016.

10. "Apply for an Employer Identification Number (EIN) Online." Internal Revenue Service. N.p., n.d. Web. 28 July 2016.

11. "Development of Human Resources - Boundless Open Textbook." Boundless. N.p., n.d. Web. 25 Aug. 2016.

12. "Visual Content and Design - Content Marketing." Content Marketing Institute. N.p., n.d. Web. 25 Aug. 2016.

13. "Markets - Home | Investopedia." Investopedia. N.p., n.d. Web. 25 Aug. 2016.

14. "Definition of Business Loans." Small Business. N.p., n.d. Web. 25 Aug. 2016.

15. "What Is Accounting? Definition and Meaning." BusinessDictionary.com. N.p., n.d. Web. 25 Aug. 2016.